Microsoft® PowerPoint® 2010:
LEVEL 1 of 3

ALEC FEHL
Asheville-Buncombe Technical Community College

LABYRINTH
LEARNING™

El Sobrante, CA

Microsoft PowerPoint 2010: Level 1
by Alec Fehl

Copyright © 2011 by Labyrinth Learning

LABYRINTH
LEARNING™

Labyrinth Learning
P.O. Box 20818
El Sobrante, California 24820
800.522.9746
On the web at lablearning.com

President:
Brian Favro

Product Development Manager:
Jason Favro

Managing Editor:
Laura A. Lionello

Production Manager:
Rad Proctor

eLearning Production Manager:
Arl S. Nadel

Editorial/Production Team:
John Barlow, Teresa Bolinger, Belinda
Breyer, Sandy Jones, PMG Media,
Sheryl Trittin

Indexing: Joanne Sprott

Interior Design:
Mark Ong, Side-by-Side Studios

Cover Design:
Words At Work

ITEM: 1-59136-320-9
ISBN-13: 978-1-59136-320-0

Manufactured in the United States of America.

10 9 8 7 6 5 4 3 2

Table of Contents

Quick Reference Tables

Preface

Microsoft® PowerPoint® 2010: Level 1 provides thorough training of PowerPoint 2010 introductory skills. This course is supported with comprehensive instructor resources and our eLab assessment and learning management tool. And, our new work-readiness exercises ensure students have the critical thinking skills necessary to succeed in today's world. After completing this course, students will be able to successfully face the challenges presented in the next book in this series, *Microsoft PowerPoint 2010: Level 2*.

Visual Conventions

This book uses many visual and typographic cues to guide students through the lessons. This page provides examples and describes the function of each cue.

`Type this text`	Anything you should type at the keyboard is printed in this typeface.
	Tips, Notes, and Warnings are used throughout the text to draw attention to certain topics.
Command→ Command→ Command, etc.	This convention indicates how to give a command from the Ribbon. The commands are written: Ribbon Tab→Command Group→Command→Subcommand.
FROM THE KEYBOARD Ctrl + S to save	These margin notes indicate shortcut keys for executing a task described in the text.

Exercise Progression

The exercises in this book build in complexity as students work through a lesson toward mastery of the skills taught.

- **Develop Your Skills** exercises are introduced immediately after concept discussions. They provide detailed, step-by-step tutorials.
- **Reinforce Your Skills** exercises provide additional hands-on practice with moderate assistance.
- **Apply Your Skills** exercises test students' skills by describing the correct results without providing specific instructions on how to achieve them.
- **Critical Thinking and Work-Readiness Skills** exercises are the most challenging. They provide generic instructions, allowing students to use their skills and creativity to achieve the results they envision.

Creating and Delivering a Presentation

LEARNING OBJECTIVES

After studying this lesson, you will be able to:

■ Apply a document theme to a new presentation

■ Insert new slides

■ Add text to a slide

■ Manage bulleted items

■ View a slide show

In this lesson, you will create a PowerPoint presentation for the iJams music distribution company. Throughout the lesson, you will be using many PowerPoint features to develop the presentation. You will be working with document themes, text layout styles, and Microsoft Word outlines. By the end of the lesson, your presentation will be ready for delivery. Equipped with the tips and techniques for a successful presentation, you will practice its delivery to the JamWorks trade show.

CASE STUDY

Creating a Presentation

iJams is an online music distribution company that sells physical CDs in addition to downloadable music. Unsigned musicians send in an existing CD or MP3 files of their original material, and then iJams duplicates the CDs on demand as orders come in and makes the MP3s available for immediate purchase or download. Musicians can also send in digital files of CD artwork, and iJams will print full color CD inserts and other supporting materials. Additionally, iJams sells promotional items branded for artists such as T-shirts, stickers, and mouse pads.

Carthic Maddix, owner of iJams, has been invited to make a presentation representing his firm to the JamWorks trade show. Carthic's goal is to introduce iJams to trade show attendees and entice them with a promotional offer. Carthic decides to use PowerPoint with his new netbook computer and video projection system to develop and deliver his presentation. Carthic chose PowcrPoint because it is easy to learn and seamlessly integrates with his other Microsoft Office applications. Carthic's dynamic speaking abilities, coupled with Power-Point's robust presentation features, are sure to win over the trade show attendees.

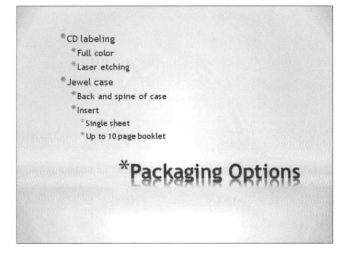

Slides from the iJams presentation

3

1.1 Presenting PowerPoint

Video Lesson   labyrinthelab.com/videos

PowerPoint 2010 is an intuitive, powerful presentation graphics program that enables you to create dynamic, multimedia presentations for a variety of functions. Whether you are developing a one-on-one presentation for your manager or a sophisticated presentation for a large group, PowerPoint provides the tools to make your presentation a success. PowerPoint allows you to project your presentation in a variety of ways. Most presentations are delivered via a computer projection display attached to a notebook computer. There are also other ways to deliver presentations. For example, you can deliver a presentation as an online broadcast over the Internet or save it as a video to be emailed or distributed on CD.

PowerPoint provides easy-to-use tools that let you concentrate on the content of your presentation instead of focusing on the design details. Using PowerPoint's built-in document themes, you can rapidly create highly effective professional presentations.

Starting PowerPoint

The method you use to start PowerPoint depends in large part on whether you intend to create a new presentation or open an existing presentation. To create a new presentation, use one of the following methods. After the PowerPoint program has started, you can begin working in the new presentation that appears.

■ Click the ⊞ button, and then choose All Programs→Microsoft Office→Microsoft Office→PowerPoint 2010.

■ Navigate to the desired document by using Windows Explorer or Computer and double-click the presentation.

DEVELOP YOUR SKILLS 1.1.1
Start PowerPoint

In this exercise, you will start PowerPoint.

1. **Click** the ⊞ button.

2. Choose **All Programs→Microsoft Office→Microsoft Office PowerPoint 2010**.
   PowerPoint will open, and the PowerPoint program window will appear.

Navigating the PowerPoint Window

Video Lesson   labyrinthelab.com/videos

The PowerPoint 2010 program window, like most other Microsoft Office programs, groups commands on the Ribbon. The following illustration provides an overview of the program window.

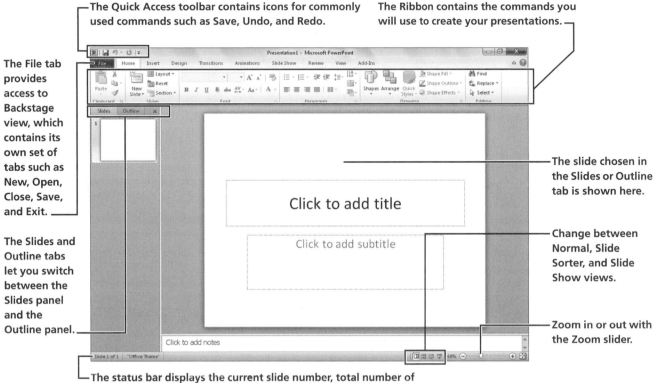

The Quick Access toolbar contains icons for commonly used commands such as Save, Undo, and Redo.

The Ribbon contains the commands you will use to create your presentations.

The File tab provides access to Backstage view, which contains its own set of tabs such as New, Open, Close, Save, and Exit.

The Slides and Outline tabs let you switch between the Slides panel and the Outline panel.

The slide chosen in the Slides or Outline tab is shown here.

Change between Normal, Slide Sorter, and Slide Show views.

Zoom in or out with the Zoom slider.

The status bar displays the current slide number, total number of slides, and the name of the document theme currently applied.

Inserting Text

PowerPoint slides have placeholders set up for you to type in. For example, the title slide currently visible on the screen has placeholders for a title and subtitle. You click in the desired placeholder to enter text on a slide. For example, to enter the title on a slide, you click in the title placeholder and then type the text. Do not press the Enter key; the placeholders are already formatted with word wrap. The placeholders also are already formatted with font and paragraph settings to make a cohesive presentation. As you will see shortly, it's easy to make changes to the formatting of slides by applying a theme.

Type a Title Slide

In this exercise, you will enter a title and subtitle for the presentation.

1. Follow these steps to add a title and subtitle:

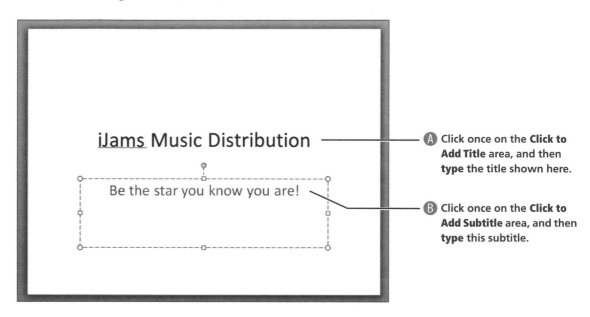

PowerPoint enters the titles. At this point you have a title slide, but it looks rather plain. This is about to change.

1.2 Using Document Themes

Video Lesson labyrinthelab.com/videos

You can use PowerPoint's built-in document themes, which provide a ready-made backdrop for your presentations, to easily format all slides in a presentation. When you use a document theme, your presentation automatically includes an attractive color scheme, consistent font style and size, and bulleted lists to synchronize with the design and style of the presentation. Document themes also position placeholders on slides for titles, text, bulleted lists, graphics, and other objects. By using document themes, you can focus on content by simply filling in the blanks as you create the presentation. You access document themes from the Themes group on the Design tab.

Choosing a Theme

There are many document themes included with PowerPoint 2010. Match the theme to the type of presentation you are giving. Keep the design appropriate to the function and the audience.

Finding Additional Themes

New themes are sent to Microsoft daily, so if you just can't find the right one, browse the Microsoft Office Online website for new themes. You can easily browse the site by selecting Design→Themes→More→Search Office Online.

This area displays the themes used in the current presentation.

Modify the colors, fonts, or effects of the current theme.

Pointing over a thumbnail displays the theme temporarily on your page. This allows you to preview the theme before you commit to it using the Live Preview feature. Click a thumbnail to apply the theme to your presentation.

Find more themes or save a modified theme.

Right-click a thumbnail to show other theme options.

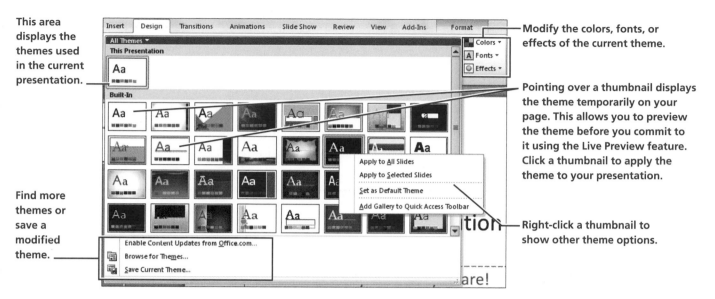

Using the PowerPoint Ribbon

The PowerPoint Ribbon is organized into nine default tabs: File, Home, Insert, Design, Transitions, Animations, Slide Show, Review, and View. Like other Office 2010 applications, additional tabs appear when certain elements on a slide are selected. These additional tabs, called contextual tabs, offer commands specific to the selected element; for example, selecting a picture on a slide results in the Picture Tools Format tab being shown. Deselecting the picture returns the Ribbon to its original state with the nine default tabs.

Each tab contains many commands, which are organized in groups. Each group is labeled across the bottom and contains a variety of buttons or button menus.

The Home tab displays several groups of buttons.

Each tab on the Ribbon contains several groups of buttons and button menus for performing various tasks.

Some groups contain a small icon in the bottom-right corner that, when clicked, displays either a dialog box or a task pane.

The Clipboard group has buttons to copy, paste, and apply the Format Painter.

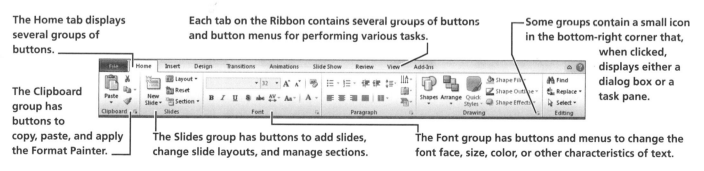

The Slides group has buttons to add slides, change slide layouts, and manage sections.

The Font group has buttons and menus to change the font face, size, color, or other characteristics of text.

DEFAULT TABS IN THE POWERPOINT RIBBON

Tab Name	General Tasks
File	Provides access to Backstage view for common tasks such as Save, Open, Close, Print, Options, and Exit.
Home	Perform standard tasks, such as copy/paste, add slides, format text, and find/search/replace.
Insert	Insert graphical elements such as shapes, pictures, clip art, charts, tables, WordArt, and media clips.
Design	Format slides with themes, colors, and backgrounds.
Transitions	Manage slide transitions.
Animations	Animate elements on a slide.
Slide Show	Create and view slide show presentations of all slides or selected slides.
Review	Proof your text with the Spelling and Thesaurus features, translate text to another language, and create comments for reviewers.
View	Change presentation views, show/hide rulers and gridlines, adjust the zoom, change the color mode, or organize multiple document windows.

QUICK REFERENCE	APPLYING A THEME
Task	**Procedure**
Apply a theme to a presentation	■ Choose Design→Themes from the Ribbon. ■ Choose a theme from the display, or click the More ⯆ button to view additional themes.

DEVELOP YOUR SKILLS 1.2.1
Apply a Document Theme

In this exercise, you will choose a document theme and apply it to the presentation.

1. Follow these steps to choose a theme for the presentation:
   Depending on your monitor resolution, you may see a different number of thumbnails in the Themes group.

Ⓐ Display the **Design** tab.

Ⓑ Locate the **Themes** command group.

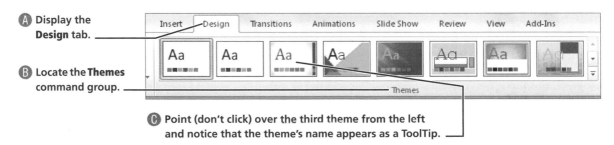

Ⓒ Point (don't click) over the third theme from the left and notice that the theme's name appears as a ToolTip.

PowerPoint displays a Live Preview of the theme on your title slide. This gives you a good idea of the overall design of the theme. Notice that the fonts and locations have changed for the title and subtitle. A different theme can radically redesign your presentation.

Throughout this book, this command will be written as follows: Choose Design→Themes→[Theme command] from the Ribbon.

2. **Point (don't click)** over several more theme thumbnails.
   You see a Live Preview of each theme on the actual slide. The themes visible on the Ribbon are just a small portion of those available, however.

3. Choose **Design→Themes→More** ⟱ as shown at right.
   PowerPoint displays all of the currently available themes. It also gives options to look for additional themes online or elsewhere on your computer.

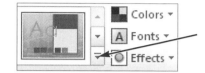

4. Follow these steps to choose a theme:

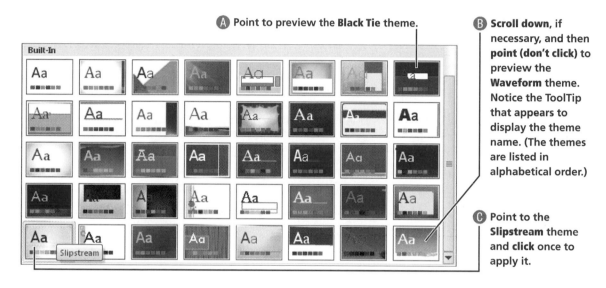

Ⓐ Point to preview the **Black Tie** theme.

Ⓑ **Scroll down,** if necessary, and then **point (don't click)** to preview the **Waveform** theme. Notice the ToolTip that appears to display the theme name. (The themes are listed in alphabetical order.)

Ⓒ Point to the **Slipstream** theme and **click** once to apply it.

PowerPoint applies the theme to your presentation.

1.3 Creating a Basic Presentation

Video Lesson   labyrinthelab.com/videos

There is more to creating a presentation than placing one slide after another. Like Carthic Maddix of iJams, you are in the process of creating an image. Choosing the appropriate slide layout, just like choosing the appropriate design, will influence how well your audience understands your message. Use the following guidelines when choosing your slide design and layout:

- **Know your audience:** Will you be speaking to accountants or artists?
- **Know your purpose:** Are you introducing a product or giving a report?
- **Know your expectations:** When the last word of this presentation has been given, how do you want your audience to respond to your facts? Are you looking for approval for a project or customers for a product?

Adding Slides

You can use two methods to add slides to a presentation:

- Choose Home→Slides→New Slide ![icon] from the Ribbon.
- Right-click a slide on the Slides panel, and then choose New Slide from the pop-up, or context, menu.

PowerPoint always places the new slide after the currently selected slide.

The Slides panel displays thumbnails of your presentation while you work in the Normal view. The Slide Sorter view, like the Slides panel, also displays thumbnails of your slides. This view can be useful when there are more slides than can fit in the Slides panel display.

DEVELOP YOUR SKILLS 1.3.1
Add a New Slide

In this exercise, you will add a new slide to the presentation and then enter content.

1. Follow these steps to add a new slide:

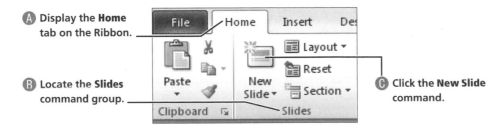

Ⓐ Display the **Home** tab on the Ribbon.

Ⓑ Locate the **Slides** command group.

Ⓒ Click the **New Slide** command.

Throughout this book, a Ribbon command like this will be written as follows: Choose Home→ Slides→New Slide ![icon] from the Ribbon.

PowerPoint adds a new slide to the presentation immediately after the title slide.

2. **Click** once in the title placeholder and then type **Our Services** as the title.

3. Click once on the **Click to Add Text** placeholder and then **type** the following list. **Tap** the `Enter` key after each list item except the last one.

   ■ **CD duplication on demand** `Enter`

   ■ **Jewel case insert printing** `Enter`

   ■ **Full service online sales** `Enter`

   ■ **Downloadable MP3 distribution**

   PowerPoint adds a bullet in front of each line.

Duplicate a Slide

Sometimes it is more efficient to duplicate a slide and then edit it rather than beginning a new slide from scratch. Slides can be duplicated via the Slides panel.

QUICK REFERENCE	DUPLICATING A SLIDE
Task	**Procedure**
Duplicate a single slide	■ Right-click the slide you wish to duplicate in the Slides panel. ■ Choose Duplicate Slide from the pop-up menu. The new slide is inserted below the original.
Duplicate multiple slides	■ `Ctrl`+click or `Shift`+click to select the slides you wish to duplicate in the Slides panel. ■ Right-click any of the selected slides and choose Duplicate Slide from the pop-up menu. The new slides are inserted below the selected slides.

Indenting Bulleted Lists

Video Lesson labyrinthelab.com/videos

When using PowerPoint, you can effortlessly create bulleted lists to outline the thrust of your presentation. The bulleted list layout is an outline of nine levels. A different indentation, and usually a different bullet character, is used for each level. The following illustration shows the Packaging Options slide you will create in the next exercise.

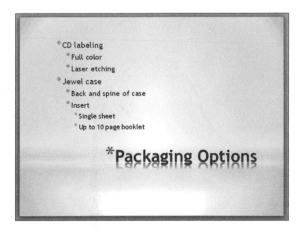

This bulleted list has three levels. Each level uses the same shaped character, but the text and bullet get smaller with each indentation.

Working with Bulleted Lists

When you use a document theme, each paragraph is automatically formatted as a bulleted list. The format includes a bullet style, indentation level, font type, and font size for each bulleted paragraph. This outline for the bulleted list is held within a placeholder or text box. The following Quick Reference table describes the various techniques that can be used with bulleted lists.

Working with List Levels

Indenting a bullet is referred to as *demoting a bullet,* or *increasing the list level.* Typically, a main bullet point has one or more sub-bullets. These sub-bullets, which are smaller than the main bullet, are created by increasing the list level. When a list level is increased, the bullets are indented toward the right. You demote a bullet by choosing the Home→Paragraph→Increase List Level button on the Ribbon. Conversely, decreasing a bullet's indent by moving it more toward the left and increasing the bullet size is referred to as *promoting a bullet*, or *decreasing the list level.* You promote a bullet by choosing the Home→Paragraph→Decrease List Level button on the Ribbon. PowerPoint supports a main bullet and up to eight sub-bullets.

QUICK REFERENCE	WORKING WITH BULLETED LISTS
Task	**Procedure**
Turn bullets on and off	■ Select the desired paragraph(s). ■ Choose Home→Paragraph→Bullets ⊞ from the Ribbon.
Promote bullets by using the Ribbon	■ Select the desired paragraph(s). ■ Choose Home→Paragraph→Decrease List Level ⊞ from the Ribbon, or use Shift + Tab .
Demote bullets by using the Ribbon	■ Select the desired paragraph(s). ■ Choose Home→Paragraph→Increase List Level ⊞ from the Ribbon, or tap the Tab key.

Create a Bulleted List

In this exercise, you will create a new slide, and then you will enter information into a multilevel bulleted list. The most efficient way to create multilevel bulleted lists is to first type the entire list.

Create the List

1. Choose **Home→Slides→New Slide** ⊞ from the Ribbon.
   PowerPoint creates a new slide after the current slide.

2. **Click** in the title placeholder and type **Packaging Options**.

3. **Click** once in the text placeholder.

4. Type **CD labeling** and tap Enter .
   PowerPoint formats the new paragraph with the same large bullet. Paragraph formats are carried to new paragraphs when you tap the Enter key.

5. **Tap** the Tab key.
   PowerPoint indents the line. It also introduces a new, slightly smaller style for the level-2 heading.

6. Type **Full color.**
PowerPoint formats the line in a smaller font too.

7. **Tap** the Enter key.
PowerPoint maintains the same level-2 heading level for the next line.

8. Type **Laser etching** and **tap** Enter.

9. While holding down the Shift key, **tap** the Tab key once.
PowerPoint promotes the new line back to level 1, which is the level of the first text line on the slide.

Manipulate Heading Levels

You can also adjust the heading level after you have typed a line.

10. **Type** the following lines:

■ **Jewel case**

■ **Back and spine of case**

11. Follow these steps to indent the last bullet:

Ⓐ **Click once** anywhere within the text line to be indented.

* Laser etching
* Jewel case
* Back and spine of case

Ⓑ Choose **Home→ Paragraph→ Increase List Level** from the Ribbon.

Paragraph

PowerPoint indents the paragraph and changes the bullet style. Demoting a paragraph makes it subordinate to the preceding paragraph.

12. Click the **Increase List Level** button three more times.
The bullet style changes and the indent increases each time you choose the command. Also, the font size and font style change with each bullet increase. These formats are determined by the Slipstream theme, on which the presentation is based.

13. Click **Home→Paragraph→Decrease List Level** from the Ribbon three times until the bullet reaches the second indentation.
With each promotion, the bullet style changes.

Indent Multiple Bullets

14. **Click** once at the end of the last line and then **tap** Enter.

15. **Type** the following new lines:

■ **Insert**

■ **Single sheet**

■ **Up to 10 page booklet**

16. Follow these steps to select the last two lines for your next command:

Ⓐ **Point** at the beginning of the text *Single sheet*, taking care that a four-pointed arrow is not visible.

* Back and spine of case
* Insert
* Single sheet
* Up to 10 page booklet

Ⓑ **Drag down** and to the right to select (highlight) the end of the last line, and then release the mouse button.

Ⓒ Ignore a context menu that may be visible for a moment. Take care not to click anywhere else on the slide before you perform the next step.

17. Choose **Home→Paragraph→Increase List Level** 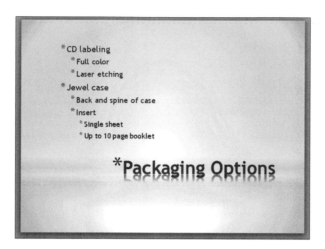 from the Ribbon.
PowerPoint indents the two selected lines.

18. **Click** anywhere outside the border to deselect the text. Your slide should match the following illustration.

Choosing the Slide Layout

Video Lesson   labyrinthelab.com/videos

There are nine slide layouts in PowerPoint 2010, one for any given situation. Slide layouts are named for the type of data they will contain. For example, the Title layout needs only a title and subtitle. The Content layout will hold other information on the slide, so it has a title and a bulleted list for points. Likewise, the Content with Caption layout is divided into three sections: title, text to one side, and an area for clip art or additional text. The slide layout organizes the information you put into the presentation by giving it a place on the slide. Use the command Home→Slides→Layout ▾ to change the layout of your slides. The new layout is applied to all selected slides. Changing layouts is easy. When you click on the new style, the layout is transferred to the selected slide.

Clicking the Layout button from the Slides group on the
Home tab allows you to apply a new layout to the selected slide(s).

Change the Slide Layout

In this exercise, you will add a new slide and then change its layout.

1. If necessary, select the **Packaging Options** slide from the Slides panel on the left side of your screen.

2. Choose **Home→Slides→New Slide** from the Ribbon.
PowerPoint adds another slide to the end of the presentation. Like the previous two slides, this one is set up to display a bulleted list.

3. Follow these steps to choose a new layout for the slide:

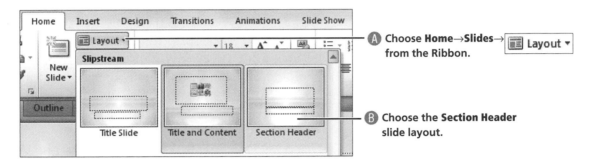

(A) Choose **Home→Slides→Layout** from the Ribbon.

(B) Choose the **Section Header** slide layout.

PowerPoint applies the new layout. Now there are two placeholders for a title and subtext.

4. Enter the following text:

   - **Title:** `Questions?`
   - **Text:** `End of our brief presentation`

Your slide should resemble the following illustration.

Saving the Presentation

Video Lesson   labyrinthelab.com/videos

FROM THE KEYBOARD
Ctrl+S to save

The byword in PowerPoint is to save early and save often. You can use the Save button on the Quick Access toolbar or use the File→Save command. If it's the first time a presentation has been saved, the Save As dialog box will appear because the file will need a name and location on your computer. You can also use the Save As dialog box to make a copy of a presentation by saving it under a new name or to a different location. If the file has already been saved, Power-Point replaces the previous version with the new edited version.

Storing Your Exercise Files

Throughout this book, you will be referred to files in your "file storage location." You can store your exercise files on various media, such as on a USB flash drive, in the Documents folder, or to a network drive at a school or company. While some figures may display files on a USB flash drive, it is assumed that you will substitute your own location for that shown in the figures. See Storing Your Exercise Files for additional information on alternative storage media. Storing Your Exercise Files is available on the student web page for this book at labyrinthelab.com/pp10.

NOTE In Windows XP, the folder is called My Documents. In Windows Vista and Windows 7, it is called Documents. Throughout this book we will use the word Documents when referring to this folder.

If you have not yet copied the student exercise files to your local file storage location, follow the instructions in Storing Your Exercise Files, located on the student web page for this book.

DEVELOP YOUR SKILLS 1.3.4
Save the Presentation

In this exercise, you will save the presentation by giving it a name and a location on your computer.

Before You Begin: Navigate to the student web page for this book at labyrinthelab.com/pp10 and see the Downloading the Student Exercise Files section of Storing Your Exercise Files for instructions on how to retrieve the student exercise files for this book and to copy them to your file storage location.

1. Click the **Save** 🖫 button on the Quick Access toolbar, as shown at right.
   PowerPoint displays the Save As dialog box because this presentation has not yet been given a filename.

2. Follow these steps to save the presentation to your file storage location:

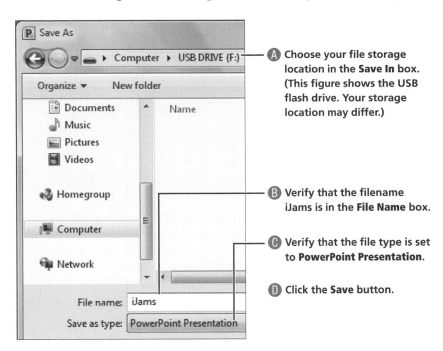

(A) Choose your file storage location in the **Save In** box. (This figure shows the USB flash drive. Your storage location may differ.)

(B) Verify that the filename iJams is in the **File Name** box.

(C) Verify that the file type is set to **PowerPoint Presentation**.

(D) Click the **Save** button.

PowerPoint saves the presentation.

Save as Video

PowerPoint 2010 has a new feature that allows you to save your presentation as a video. This is helpful if you want to distribute your presentation to others without requiring them to have PowerPoint or other special software. The video files are saved in the Windows Media Video (.wmv) format and are playable on any Windows computer. When saving as a video, be patient as it takes some time to convert your presentation to the video format.

The status bar at the bottom of the PowerPoint window shows the video conversion progress.

You can cancel the conversion at any time.

The video version of a presentation can be 15 times larger than the original PowerPoint file. Be aware of the file size before you try to email a video to someone.

QUICK REFERENCE	SAVING A PRESENTATION AS A VIDEO
Task	**Procedure**
Save a presentation as a video	■ Choose File→Save & Send→Create a Video.
	■ Choose the quality setting and whether or not to use slide timings.
	■ Set the number of seconds to display each slide.
	■ Click Create Video, choose a save location, and click Save.
	■ Wait as the video is converted.

1.4 Delivering the Slide Show

Video Lesson   labyrinthelab.com/videos

The slides are created, and the presentation is complete. The first phase of the presentation development is over. The next phase, delivering the presentation, is just beginning. Before you stand before an audience, familiarize yourself with the following tips.

Delivery Tips

It is not only what you say, it is how you say it that makes the difference between an engaging and an unsuccessful presentation. Lead your audience. Help them to focus on the message of your presentation, not on you as the presenter. Use the following *PEER* guidelines to deliver an effective presentation:

- *Pace:* Maintain a moderate pace. Speaking too fast will exhaust your audience, and speaking too slowly may put them to sleep. Carry your audience with you as you talk.

- *Emphasis:* Pause for emphasis. As you present, use a brief pause to emphasize your point. The pause you take will give your audience time to absorb the message.

- *Eye contact:* Address your audience. Always face your audience while speaking. A common mistake is to speak while walking or facing the projection screen. Don't waste all of the work you have done in the presentation by losing the interest of your audience now. If you are speaking from a lectern or desk, resist the temptation to lean on it. Stand tall, make eye contact, and look directly at your audience.

- *Relax:* You are enthusiastic and want to convey that tone to the audience. However, when you speak, avoid fast movement, pacing, and rushed talking. Your audience will be drawn to your movements and miss the point. Remember that the audience is listening to you to learn; this material may be old hat to you, but it's new to them. So speak clearly, maintain a steady pace, and stay calm.

Navigating Through a Slide Show

FROM THE KEYBOARD

Spacebar or → to advance a slide

Backspace or ← to back up a slide

You can use the mouse and/or simple keyboard commands to move through a slide show. This is often the easiest way to navigate from one slide to the next.

The Slide Show Toolbar

The Slide Show toolbar is your navigator during the slide show. Notice that the Slide Show toolbar has options to go to the next and previous slides and to end the slide show. The Slide Show toolbar also lets you use a pen tool to draw on the slide and make other enhancements. However, use of this toolbar is unnecessary when you present a simple slide show like this one.

QUICK REFERENCE	USING BASIC SLIDE SHOW NAVIGATION
Task	**Procedure**
Advance a slide	■ Click once with the mouse, or
	■ Tap the Spacebar, →, Page Down, or Enter key.
Back up a slide	■ Tap the Backspace, Page Up, or ← key.
Display the Slide Show toolbar	■ Move the mouse around on the screen for a moment.

Run the Slide Show

In this exercise, you will navigate through your slide show.

Before You Begin: The iJams presentation should be open in PowerPoint.

1. **Click** once on the first slide in the **Slides** panel as shown at right.
   The Slides panel along the left side of the PowerPoint window is a handy way to navigate to various slides. You will start your presentation by displaying the Title slide.

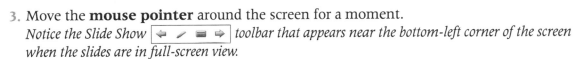

2. Choose **Slide Show→Start Slide Show→ From Beginning** from the Ribbon.
   PowerPoint displays your title slide in full-screen view. All toolbars and other screen objects are hidden from view.

3. Move the **mouse pointer** around the screen for a moment.
   Notice the Slide Show ⟸ ⁄ ▤ ⟹ *toolbar that appears near the bottom-left corner of the screen when the slides are in full-screen view.*

4. Click the **mouse pointer** anywhere on the screen to move to the next slide.

5. **Tap** the [Page Down] key twice and then **tap** [Page Up] twice by using the keys near the main keyboard (not the keys on the numeric keypad).
   PowerPoint displays the next or previous slide each time you tap these keys.

Manipulate the Slide Show Toolbar

6. Click the **Slide Options** button on the Slide Show toolbar. Choose **Go to Slide→Packaging Options**.
   In the Go to Slide menu, your entire presentation is outlined by title. Simply choose the slide you want to see.

7. Choose **Go to Slide→iJams Music Distribution**.
   As you can see, there are many ways to navigate slides in an electronic slide show.

End the Slide Show

8. Continue to click anywhere on the screen until the last slide appears (the Questions slide).

9. **Click** once on the last slide.
   The screen turns to a black background, with a small note at the top.

10. **Click** anywhere on the black screen to exit the slide show and return to the main PowerPoint window.

11. Feel free to practice running your slide show again.

12. When you have finished, click the **Save** 🖫 button to save any changes to your presentation.

13. Choose **File→Close** to close the presentation.

1.5 Getting Help

Video Lesson labyrinthelab.com/videos

PowerPoint, like many other software programs, has so many features it is unlikely you will learn and remember everything about it at once. That is where PowerPoint Help comes in. You can use the help system to learn to perform specific tasks or browse general information about a variety of categories.

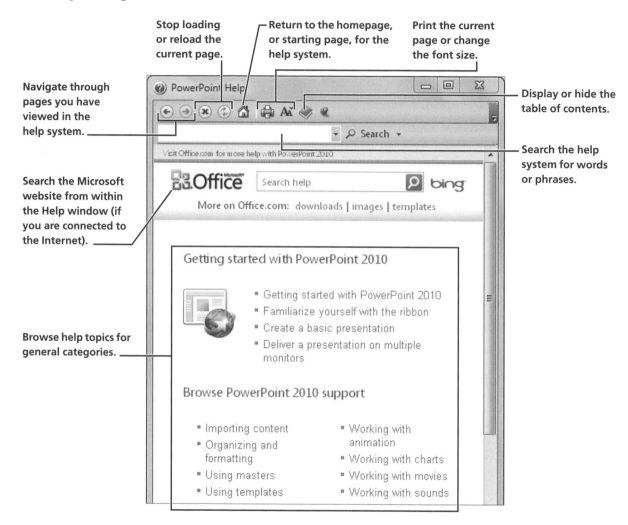

Stop loading or reload the current page.

Return to the homepage, or starting page, for the help system.

Print the current page or change the font size.

Navigate through pages you have viewed in the help system.

Display or hide the table of contents.

Search the Microsoft website from within the Help window (if you are connected to the Internet).

Search the help system for words or phrases.

Browse help topics for general categories.

Online and Offline Help

If you are connected to the Internet when you open the PowerPoint Help window, PowerPoint connects to the Microsoft website and displays the most up-to-date help content. If you are not connected to the Internet, offline help topics that were installed when PowerPoint was installed are displayed.

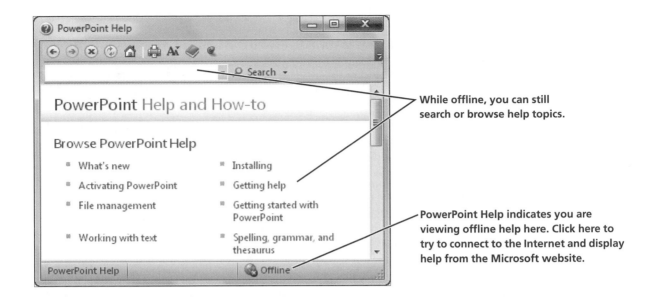

While offline, you can still search or browse help topics.

PowerPoint Help indicates you are viewing offline help here. Click here to try to connect to the Internet and display help from the Microsoft website.

| QUICK REFERENCE | USING POWERPOINT HELP |

Task	Procedure
Start PowerPoint Help	■ Click the Microsoft PowerPoint Help button 🔘 on the right side of the Ribbon.
	■ Tap F1 on the keyboard.
	■ Choose File→Help and then click one of the options in the Support section.

DEVELOP YOUR SKILLS 1.5.1

Use PowerPoint Help

In this exercise, you will use the PowerPoint Help system.

Search for Help

1. Click the **Microsoft PowerPoint Help** 🔘 button on the right side of the Ribbon to display the Help window.

2. Follow these steps to search for help:

Ⓐ Click in the **Search** box and type `font color`.

Ⓑ Tap Enter.

Ⓒ Click any of the results to view help about the search topic. Note that your results may differ and your computer may not match the figure.

Ⓓ Click **Home** to return to the PowerPoint Help start page.

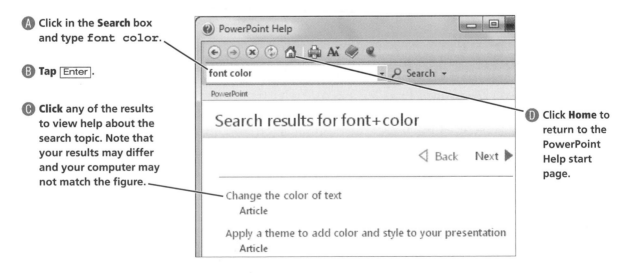

Use the Table of Contents

3. Follow these steps to browse for help using the table of contents:

Ⓐ Click **Show Table of Contents** to display the Table of Contents pane.

Ⓑ If necessary, scroll down until you see the **Working with Text** topic.

Ⓒ Click **Working with Text** to display the help topics for that category. Your screen may differ from the figure.

Ⓓ Click any of the topics to read them.

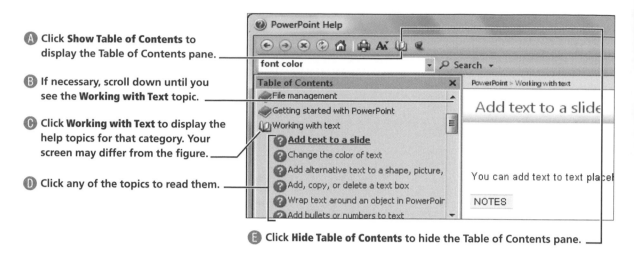

Ⓔ Click **Hide Table of Contents** to hide the Table of Contents pane.

4. **Close** X the PowerPoint Help window.

5. Choose **File→Exit** to close PowerPoint.

1.6 Concepts Review

Concepts Review   labyrinthelab.com/pp10

To check your knowledge of the key concepts introduced in this lesson, complete the Concepts Review quiz by going to the URL listed above. If your classroom is using Labyrinth eLab, you may complete the Concepts Review quiz from within your eLab course.

Reinforce Your Skills

Create a Presentation

In this exercise, you will create a presentation for the Tropical Getaways travel service. The presentation will be used to sell potential customers a tropical getaway to paradise. The managers of Tropical Getaways will be delivering the presentation to an audience of more than 40 people.

1. **Start** the PowerPoint program.
   A new presentation appears when PowerPoint starts. To gain practice creating a new presentation, you will close that and create a new one.

2. Follow these steps to close the existing presentation:

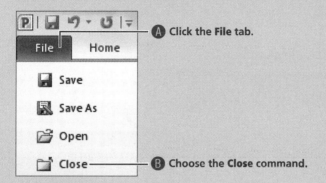

   A Click the **File** tab.

   B Choose the **Close** command.

   The presentation closes.

3. Choose **File** →**New**.
   The New Presentation window appears.

4. Double-click the **Blank Presentation** choice.
   A new presentation with a single slide is created.

Apply a Document Theme

5. Choose **Design**→**Themes**, and choose the **Civic** theme.
   PowerPoint applies the theme to your presentation.

6. Click in the **Title** placeholder and **type** the title **Tropical Getaways**.

7. Click in the **Subtitle** placeholder and **type** the subtitle **Adventures in Paradise**.
   As you type, the text is converted to uppercase because that is a design element of this particular document theme.

8. **Save** your presentation as **rs-Tropical Getaways** on your file storage location.

Set Up Another Slide

9. Choose **Home→Slides→New Slide** 🖼 from the Ribbon.
   A single-column, bulleted list slide is added to the presentation. Notice that the Civic document theme is applied to the new slide.

10. Choose **Home→Slides→** 🖼 **Layout ▾** **→Two Content** from the Ribbon.
    A new two-column layout is applied to the slide.

11. Click in the **Title** placeholder and **type** the title **Most Popular Destinations**.

12. Add the following text to the bulleted list on the left:
    - **Tahiti**
    - **Maui**
    - **Oahu**
    - **Cancun**

13. Add the following text to the bulleted list on the right:
    - **Caribbean**
    - **Fiji**
    - **Singapore**
    - **Australia**

    After you finish typing, your slide should look similar to the following illustration.

14. **Save** 💾 your presentation.

Set Up the Remaining Slides

15. Choose **Home→Slides→New Slide** 🖼 from the Ribbon.
    A third slide is added to the presentation. The new slide has the same Two Content layout as the previous slide.

16. In the **Title** placeholder, enter the phrase **Complete Packages**.

17. In the first bullet of the left bulleted list, enter the phrase **Packages Include** and **tap** ⌷Enter⌷.

18. Choose **Home→Paragraph→Increase List Level** 🔧 from the Ribbon.
    The bullet is indented and a new bullet character is applied by the design template.

19. Add the following text to the bulleted list on the left:
    - **Airfare**
    - **Lodging**
    - **Rental car**
    - **Activities**

20. In the first bullet of the bulleted list on the right, enter the phrase **Low Prices** and **tap** `Enter`.

21. Choose **Home→Paragraph→Increase List Level** 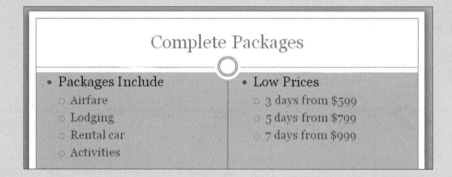 from the Ribbon.
    The bullet is indented, and a new bullet character is applied by the design template.

22. Add the following text to the bulleted list on the right:
    - **3 days from $599**
    - **5 days from $799**
    - **7 days from $999**

    After you finish typing, your slide should look similar to the following illustration.

Complete Packages

- Packages Include
    - Airfare
    - Lodging
    - Rental car
    - Activities
- Low Prices
    - 3 days from $599
    - 5 days from $799
    - 7 days from $999

23. Choose **Home→Slides→New Slide** to add a fourth slide to your presentation.

24. Choose **Home→Slides→ Layout ▾→Title and Content** to change the slide layout to the Title and Content layout.

25. Enter the title **Travel Now and Save!**

26. **Type** the following bullet points in the text box:
    - **Package 1**
    - **5 days in Oahu**
    - **$429 per person**
    - **Package 2**
    - **7 days in Tahiti**
    - **$1,299 per person**

27. Select the *5 days in Oahu* and *$429 per person* paragraphs and **increase** their list level.

28. Select the *7 days in Tahiti* and *$1,299 per person* paragraphs and **increase** their list level.
After you finish typing, your slide should look similar to the following illustration.

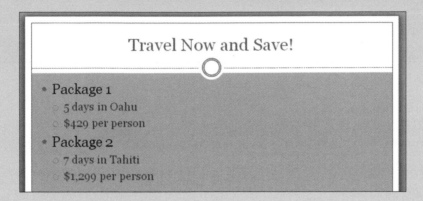

29. Choose **Home→Slides→New Slide** to add the final slide to the presentation.

30. Type **Tropical Getaways** for the title.

31. Type the following in the text box:

■ **Angelica Escobedo**

■ **(310) 544-8870**

32. Click the **dashed border** around the text box so it turns solid, and choose **Home→Paragraph→Bullets** to remove the bullets.
The bullets are removed from all paragraphs in the text box.

33. Select **Home→Paragraph→Center** 📄 from the Ribbon to center the text on the slide.
After you finish typing, your slide should look similar to the following illustration.

34. Save 💾 the presentation.
Leave the presentation open if you will continue to the next exercise.

Deliver a Slide Show

In this exercise, you will practice delivering the Tropical Getaways presentation.

Before You Begin: The rs-Tropical Getaways presentation created in Reinforce Your Skills 1.1 should be open in PowerPoint.

1. Select the first slide from the **Slides** panel on the left side of your screen.

2. Choose **Slide Show→Start Slide Show→From Beginning** 📺 from the Ribbon.
   The Title slide will occupy your whole screen as the slide show starts.

3. Walk through the presentation by **clicking** each slide until the presentation is ended.

4. **Click** once more to return to the PowerPoint program window.

5. Choose **Slide Show→Start Slide Show→From Beginning** 📺 from the Ribbon to start the slide show again.

6. After the slide show begins, **position** the mouse pointer at the bottom-left corner of the screen to display the **Slide Show** toolbar.

7. Click the **Slide Options** button as shown at right on the Slide Show toolbar.

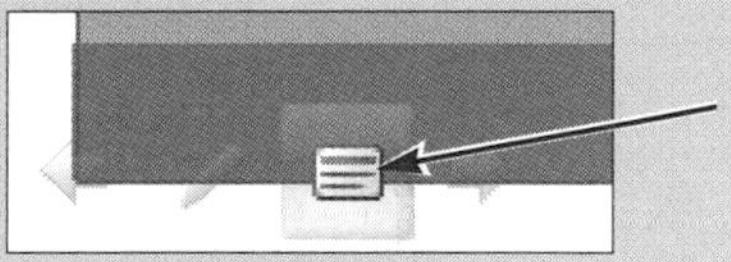

8. Choose **Go to Slide→Travel Now and Save!**
   Notice that the Go to Slide drop-down menu displays the title of each slide in your presentation.

9. Use the **Slide Options** button on the Slide Show toolbar to end the slide show by choosing **End Show**.

10. **Save** and **close** the presentation, and then **close** the PowerPoint program window.

Apply Your Skills

Create a Presentation

In this exercise, you will create a presentation for Classic Cars. Classic Cars is an organization devoted to tracking, categorizing, and preserving classic automobiles. The presentation will be given to members of the Classic Cars organization at the annual Classic Cars convention.

1. **Start** PowerPoint.
   A new presentation is started for you automatically.

2. Apply the **Horizon** design document theme, as shown in the following illustration.

3. Add the following text to the **Title** slide:
   - **Title:** `Classic Cars`
   - **Subtitle:** `2010 Convention Highlights`

4. Add a second slide with the following text:

Title	Seminar Topics
Bulleted paragraphs	■ Restoration Techniques
	■ Preservation Techniques
	■ Locating Vehicles
	■ Success Stories
	■ Winning Competitions

5. Add a third slide with the following text:

Title	Collections on Display
Bulleted paragraphs	■ James McGee - 1950s Corvettes
	■ Beth Zelinko - Classic Fords
	■ Ricardo Campos - Thunderbirds
	■ Ava Peters - Corvairs

6. Add a fourth slide and change its layout to a **Two Content** layout. Add the following text:

Title	Door Prizes
Left bulleted paragraphs	■ Car care items
	■ Gift certificates
	■ Floor mats
	■ Waxes and polishes
	■ Magazines
Right bulleted paragraphs	■ Entertainment
	■ Las Vegas vacation
	■ Sporting events
	■ Movie tickets
	■ Dinners

7. Select all but the first bullet in the **left** text box and increase the list level.

8. Select all but the first bullet in the **right** text box and increase the list level.
After you finish, the slide should appear similar to the following illustration.

9. Add a final slide to the presentation and apply the **Title and Content** layout.
  ■ **Title: The 2010 Convention**
  ■ **Text: Enjoy the Ride...**

10. Save the presentation as **as-Classic Cars** to your file storage location.

Critical Thinking & Work-Readiness Skills

In the course of working through the following Microsoft Office-based Critical Thinking exercises, you will also be utilizing various work-readiness skills, some of which are listed next to each exercise. Go to labyrinthelab.com/ workreadiness to learn more about the work-readiness skills.

1.1 Create a Basic Presentation

WORK-READINESS SKILLS APPLIED

- Thinking creatively
- Making decisions
- Reasoning

Carthic decides on three points to make in his iJams conference presentation: 1) Why he founded iJams (a need for a focused website, his industry experience, encouragement from well known musicians); 2) How iJams is different (only covers independent bands, has expert editors, features exclusive downloads); and 3) The special trade show offer (download five songs free by using the code). Open PowerPoint and create a new blank presentation. Use the New Slide command to create one slide for each of the three main points, condensing supporting points to short phrases or single words in a bulleted list. Insert a title slide. Save your presentation as **ct-iJams Points** to your Lesson 01 folder.

1.2 Format a Presentation

WORK-READINESS SKILLS APPLIED

- Thinking creatively
- Interpreting and communicating information
- Speaking

Open ct-iJams Points, if necessary, and use the Save As command to save it with the new name **ct-Formatted**. Experiment with slide layouts, document themes, and indenting bulleted lists. Save the three "best" (in your opinion) solutions as separate files: **ct-Formatted1**, **ct-Formatted2**, and **ct-Formatted3**. View them as slide shows with a group. Discuss which solution is most effective and why. If working alone, type your responses in a Word document named **ct-Questions** saved to your Lesson 01 folder.

1.3 Change and Practice a Presentation

WORK-READINESS SKILLS APPLIED

- Reasoning
- Thinking creatively
- Participating as a member of a team

Open ct-Formatted from the previous exercise. Add a slide with an endorsement that's just come in from a famous musician. Mike Smith of the Rolling Beetles says, "iJams is awesome! I use it almost every day. Congratulations, Carthic!" Place the new slide in what you consider an appropriate place. Be prepared to explain why you put the slide where you did. Now view the presentation as a slide show. Practice the presentation with a group in class, and get feedback, especially on how the slide-to-slide transitions are affected by the addition of a slide. Save the file and close PowerPoint.

Designing the Presentation

LEARNING OBJECTIVES

After studying this lesson, you will be able to:

- Copy and move text
- Use Outline view to create, move, and delete slides and edit text
- Create a presentation from a Microsoft Word outline
- Format and align text and adjust character spacing and line spacing
- Use the Slide Sorter view to rearrange the order of slides
- Use the new Sections feature to manage multiple slides
- Print a presentation

In this lesson, you will build on the fundamental design of the iJams presentation. You will establish a consistent style throughout the presentation and format and organize the text. You will add slides to your presentation from the Outline panel and manipulate your completed presentation by using the Slide Sorter view and Sections. You will also create a presentation from a Microsoft Word outline. Lastly, working with the printing function of PowerPoint 2010, you will examine page setup, print preview, print setup, and the output formats options.

Designing a Presentation

Now that the initial slides of the iJams presentation are complete, Carthic Maddix is wondering how he can polish the presentation for the JamWorks trade show. Carthic confers with his administrative assistant, Aurelia, who will be formatting the presentation for him. In turning over the presentation to Aurelia, Carthic asks her to make sure that the style is consistent throughout the presentation. He also wants her to check that the slides are in a logical sequence so the presentation is clear. Carthic knows that Aurelia is an expert in PowerPoint. He is confident in her ability to make the presentation shine.

* Audio CDs
* Downloadable MP3s
* T-shirts
* Baseball caps
* Stickers

* Pencils
* Key chains
* Posters
* Mugs
* Mouse pads

* **Products and Promotional Items**

Sample of slide formatted with a layout Microsoft calls the Two Content layout

2.1 Working with Slides

Video Lesson   labyrinthelab.com/videos

As your presentation progresses and you insert additional slides, you may want to change the layout or the order of your slides. For example, some slides may require two columns of bulleted text while others require only one. PowerPoint makes it easy to change the order of slides using the Slide Sorter view.

Copying Text and Objects

FROM THE KEYBOARD
Ctrl+X to cut
Ctrl+C to copy
Ctrl+V to paste

You can move and copy text and objects by using drag and drop or the Cut, Copy, and Paste commands. It is usually most efficient to use drag and drop if you are moving or copying text or objects within a slide or to another slide that is visible on the screen. Drag and drop is also effective for rearranging slides. Cut, Copy, and Paste are most efficient when moving or copying to a location not visible on the current screen.

QUICK REFERENCE	MOVING AND COPYING TEXT AND OBJECTS
Task	**Procedure**
Drag and drop	■ Select the desired text or click an object, such as a placeholder box.
	■ Drag to move the text or object to the desired location. Press the Ctrl key while dragging if you wish to copy.
Right-drag and drop	■ Select the desired text or click an object, such as a placeholder box.
	■ Use the right mouse button to drag the text or object to the desired location.
	■ Release the mouse button at the desired location and choose Move, Copy, or Cancel from the context menu.
Cut, copy, and paste	■ Select the desired text or click an object, such as a placeholder box.
	■ Click the Cut button or use Ctrl+X to cut the item. Click the Copy button or use Ctrl+C to copy the item.
	■ Navigate to the desired slide and click at the location where you want to paste.
	■ Click the Paste button or use Ctrl+V to paste the item.

DEVELOP YOUR SKILLS 2.1.1
Add a New Slide to a Presentation

In this exercise, you will add a new slide to a presentation, enter a bulleted list, and change the layout of the slide. You can always change the layout for a slide after the slide has been created.

1. **Start** PowerPoint.

2. **Open** the iJams Design presentation from the Lesson 2 folder in your file storage location.

Add a Slide

3. Select the **Our Services** slide from the Slides panel on the left side of your screen.
   The Our Services slide appears. New slides are placed after the selected slide.

4. Choose **Home→Slides→New Slide** 📋 from the Ribbon.

5. **Click** in the Title placeholder and type **Products and Promotional Items**.

6. **Click** in the bulleted list placeholder and **type** the following bulleted list:

   - **Audio CDs**
   - **Downloadable MP3s**
   - **T-shirts**
   - **Baseball caps**
   - **Stickers**
   - **Pencils**
   - **Key chains**
   - **Posters**
   - **Mugs**
   - **Mouse pads**

   When you begin typing Posters, PowerPoint will reformat all of the bullets with a smaller font size so that all the bullets can fit into the box. As you type the last bullet point, Mouse pads, the font gets even smaller. Because a long list of bullets can be overwhelming, limit the number of bullets to three to six on a slide. If there is more information, consider breaking the list into two columns. In the next two steps, you will use this technique by choosing a different layout for the slide.

Change the Slide Layout and Move Text

7. Follow these steps to change the slide layout:

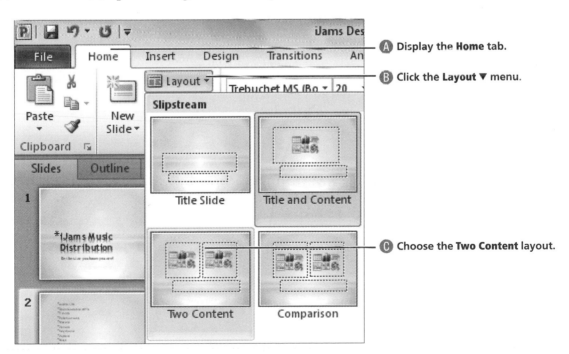

PowerPoint applies the Two Content layout to the current slide.

8. Follow these steps to move the last five bullets to the second box:

Ⓐ **Select** the last five bulleted paragraphs by dragging the mouse pointer over the text, and then **release** the mouse button.

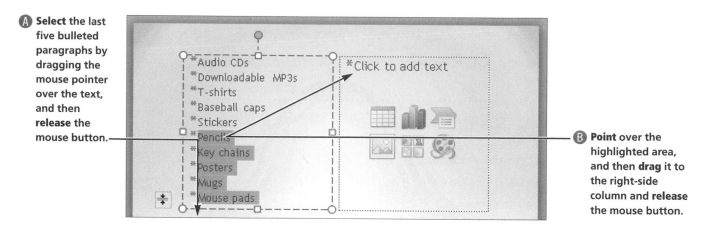

Ⓑ **Point** over the highlighted area, and then **drag** it to the right-side column and **release** the mouse button.

This command moves the last five bulleted paragraphs into the right-side content area.

9. Click the **Save** 🖫 button to save the changes to your presentation.

2.2 Working with Outlines

Video Lesson labyrinthelab.com/videos

Although you have been working primarily in the slide to add or format text, the Outline panel is an alternative way to add, remove, and move text. The Outline panel is a useful interface to organize or structure your presentation.

Using the Outline Panel

The Outline panel helps you to edit and reorganize your slides. The Outline panel is available on the left side of your screen if you are in Normal view. You can type directly in the Outline panel to add or edit text on a slide. You can also select text from the Outline panel and format it with the standard formatting commands on the Ribbon. Any changes made in the Outline panel are immediately reflected in the actual slide.

You can choose a slide in an outline by clicking the slide icon or by clicking on any text within the slide. The selected slide is displayed in the main portion of the window.

Double-click a slide icon to collapse the text contents. Double-click again to expand the contents.

Switch to the Outline panel by clicking the Outline tab.

Ribbon commands, such as Font Size or Increase List Level, can be applied to a selection in the Outline tab. You don't have to make a selection on the large slide to edit text.

You can edit text directly on the Outline tab without having to make a selection on the large slide itself.

The content of left and right content boxes is indicated by the boxes 1 and 2.

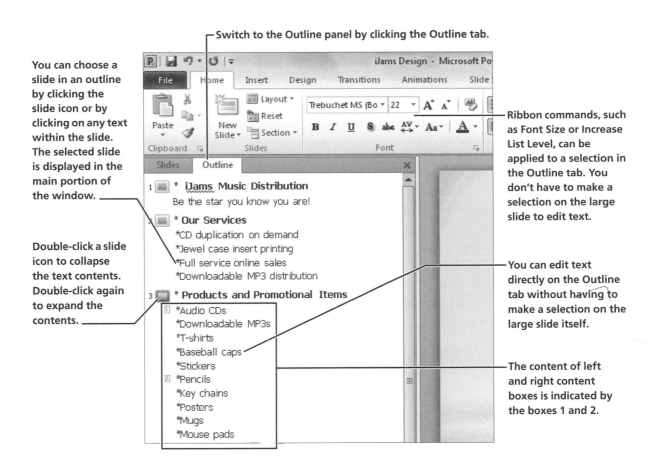

QUICK REFERENCE · WORKING WITH OUTLINES

Task	Procedure
Select text in an outline	Drag over the desired text in the Outline panel.
Select an entire slide	Click the slide icon in the Outline panel.
Expand or collapse a slide	Double-click the slide icon in the Outline panel.
Add a new slide	Place the mouse pointer in the last group of bulleted paragraphs on a slide and press Ctrl+Enter.
Delete a slide	Right-click any text within a slide in the Outline panel, and then choose Delete Slide from the context menu.

Add a Slide in the Outline Panel

In this exercise, you will work with the Outline panel to add and move slides.

1. Follow these steps to select a slide while in the Outline panel:

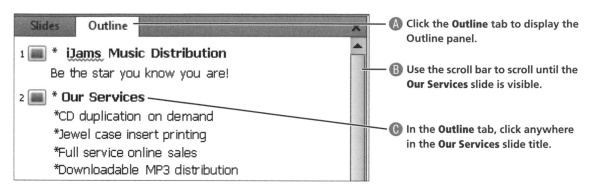

(A) Click the **Outline** tab to display the Outline panel.

(B) Use the scroll bar to scroll until the **Our Services** slide is visible.

(C) In the **Outline** tab, click anywhere in the **Our Services** slide title.

2. **Press** Ctrl + Enter.
   The cursor moves to the next box in the slide.

3. **Press** Ctrl + Enter.
   PowerPoint creates a new slide below the selected slide.

4. Follow these steps to add text to the new slide while in the Outline panel:

(A) Type **Current Artists** directly in the Outline tab. As you type this title in the Outline tab, the text also appears in the large slide in the main portion of your window.

(B) **Press** Ctrl + Enter to move to the bulleted paragraph box.

(C) **Type** the three bulleted paragraphs shown here, tapping Enter after each paragraph.

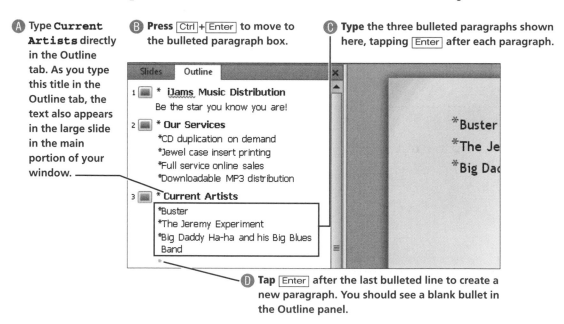

(D) **Tap** Enter after the last bulleted line to create a new paragraph. You should see a blank bullet in the Outline panel.

PowerPoint adds a new slide to the presentation whenever the mouse pointer is positioned within the last box on a slide and the Ctrl + Enter keystroke combination is issued.

At this point, you should have a new bulleted paragraph visible in the outline below the Big Daddy Ha-ha paragraph.

Add Two New Slides

5. Follow these steps to promote a paragraph to make a new slide:

   ■ Make sure the **insertion point** is on the blank bulleted paragraph in the outline as shown at right.

   ■ Choose **Home→Paragraph→Decrease List Level** from the Ribbon.

   PowerPoint promotes the bulleted paragraph to create a new slide.

6. Type **New Artist Specials** and **tap** [Enter].
   Notice that tapping [Enter] *created a new slide. You must use the* [Ctrl]+[Enter] *keystroke combination to add a bulleted paragraph after a title slide. However, you will fix this by demoting the new slide in the next step.*

7. Choose **Home→Paragraph→Increase List Level** [≣] button from the Ribbon.
   The new slide created when you tapped [Enter] *in step 6 has been converted to a bullet under the New Artist Specials title.*

8. Complete the new slide in the outline as shown, **tapping** [Enter] after each paragraph (including the last paragraph).

Bulleted Paragraphs	■ **25% discount on CD duplication** [Enter]
	■ **Five free T-shirts** [Enter]
	■ **10% discount on promotional items** [Enter]
	■ **Valid until July 20** [Enter]

9. Choose **Home→Paragraph→Decrease List Level** [≣] from the Ribbon to promote the new paragraph that follows the Valid Until July 20 paragraph and convert it into a new slide.

10. Type **Contact Us**, and then use [Ctrl]+[Enter] to create a bullet below the title you just typed.

11. Taking care **not** to tap [Enter] after the last bullet in this slide, complete the new slide as shown.

Bulleted Paragraphs	■ **Call**
	■ **(510) 235-7788**
	■ **Or**
	■ **Email us at**
	■ **iJams@example.com**

   You will format this slide in a later activity.

Collapsing and Expanding Slides

Video Lesson labyrinthelab.com/videos

As the Outline panel grows, it can be difficult to manage your slides when all the bulleted text is showing. PowerPoint lets you collapse slides so that only the title is visible. This makes it easier to manage your slides because more slides will be visible in the Outline panel.

The same presentation in Outline view with all slides expanded and all slides collapsed

---

DEVELOP YOUR SKILLS 2.2.2

Use the Context Menu on the Outline Panel

In this exercise, you will use the context menu from the Outline panel.

1. Follow these steps to explore the Outline panel:

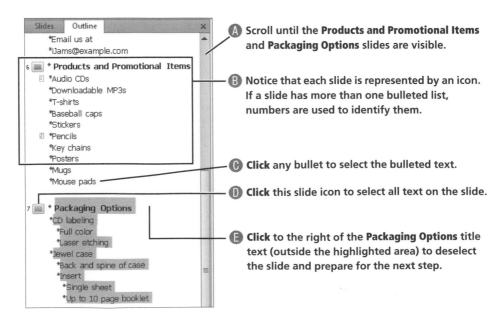

Ⓐ Scroll until the **Products and Promotional Items** and **Packaging Options** slides are visible.

Ⓑ Notice that each slide is represented by an icon. If a slide has more than one bulleted list, numbers are used to identify them.

Ⓒ **Click** any bullet to select the bulleted text.

Ⓓ **Click** this slide icon to select all text on the slide.

Ⓔ **Click** to the right of the **Packaging Options** title text (outside the highlighted area) to deselect the slide and prepare for the next step.

2. **Double-click** the slide icon 🖳 to the left of the Products and Promotional Items title.
   The bulleted paragraphs beneath the title are collapsed and hidden.

3. **Double-click** the slide icon 🖳 to the left of the Products and Promotional Items title again.
   The bulleted paragraphs beneath the title are expanded and are once again visible.

4. **Right-click** anywhere in the Outline panel and choose **Collapse→Collapse All** from the context menu.
   All bulleted paragraphs are collapsed and hidden. Only the slide titles remain visible.

5. **Right-click** anywhere in the Outline panel and choose **Expand→Expand All** from the context menu.
   All bulleted paragraphs are expanded and are once again visible.

Move a Slide

The easiest way to move a slide in an outline is to first collapse all slides. Then you can click on the desired slide title and drag it to its new position.

6. **Right-click** anywhere in the Outline panel and choose **Collapse→Collapse All**.

7. If necessary, **scroll up** until all slide icons and titles are visible in the outline.

8. Follow these steps to move a slide:

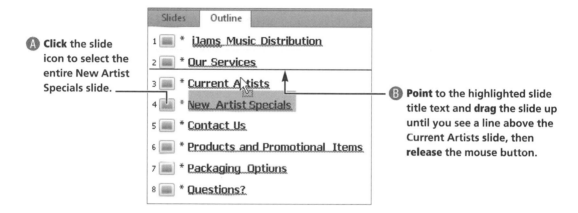

Ⓐ Click the slide icon to select the entire New Artist Specials slide.

Ⓑ Point to the highlighted slide title text and **drag** the slide up until you see a line above the Current Artists slide, then **release** the mouse button.

The New Artists Specials slide appears above the Current Artists slide.

9. Using this same method, move the Packaging Options slide to the second position, just below the Title slide.

Deleting Slides

Video Lesson   labyrinthelab.com/videos

You can delete a slide in an outline by clicking the slide icon to select the entire slide and then tapping the [Delete] key. Likewise, slides can be deleted in Normal and Slide Sorter views by choosing the desired slide(s) and tapping [Delete]. If you inadvertently delete a slide, you can use the Undo button on the Quick Access toolbar to undo the latest action and restore the deleted slide. If you later decide that you want to keep the change, click the Redo button on the Quick Access toolbar to go back to the previous action.

DEVELOP YOUR SKILLS 2.2.3
Delete a Slide from the Outline

In this exercise, you will delete a slide by using the Outline tab.

1. **Right-click** anywhere in the Outline panel and choose **Expand→Expand All**.

2. **Click** the Current Artists slide icon ▣ (not the title text) to select the entire slide.

3. **Tap** the [Delete] key on the keyboard to delete the slide.
   A faded bullet may appear at the end of the previous slide. This is PowerPoint readying itself for additional text. The ghost bullet will not display on the slide itself.

4. Using this same method, **delete** the Questions slide.

5. **Save** your presentation and then choose **File→Close** to close it.

2.3 Working with Word Integration

Video Lesson   labyrinthelab.com/videos

Microsoft Word is an excellent word processing program that integrates with PowerPoint. Outlines created in Word can easily be converted to a PowerPoint presentation.

Creating a Presentation Outline in Word

Word's powerful outlining tool makes setting up and modifying outlines easy. You can create an outline in Word and import it to PowerPoint. To use Word outlines in PowerPoint, you must apply the appropriate styles to the paragraphs in the Word document prior to importing the outline. PowerPoint converts the Word outline by using these rules:

■ All Level 1 paragraphs translate to Titles in a PowerPoint slide.
■ All Level 2 paragraphs translate to Level 1 Body Bullets in a PowerPoint slide.
■ All Level 3 paragraphs translate to Level 2 Body Bullets in a PowerPoint slide.

Once a Word outline is imported into PowerPoint, you can promote or demote the bullets, apply layouts and a design template, and make other enhancements.

This Word outline...

...creates these PowerPoint slides.

Create a Presentation and Import a Word Outline

In this exercise, you will start a new iJams presentation, create an outline in Word, and modify the resulting presentation.

Create an Outline in Word

1. **Start** Word and a blank document will be displayed.
   In the next few steps, you will type and apply Word styles to paragraphs.

2. With the blank document open, choose **View→Document Views→Outline** from the Ribbon to switch to Outline view.

3. Type **iJams Music Distribution** Enter.

4. **Type** Tab **A Year of Success** Enter.
   Typing Tab *increases the list level and creates a Level 2 style.*

5. **Type** Shift+Tab **Online Downloads** Enter.
   Typing Shift+Tab *decreases the list level and returns the text to a Level 1 style.*

6. **Type** the following to create Level 2 style text that will be converted in PowerPoint to text bullets:

   Tab **MP3 sales exceed $1M** Enter

   350 thousand new user accounts Enter

   Shift+Tab

   Pressing Shift+Tab *returns you to a Level 1 style and you are ready to continue typing the rest of the outline.*

7. Continue **typing** the outline as follows:

`Promotional Items` [Enter]

[Tab] `T-shirt sales exceed $500k` [Enter]

`Total promotional item sales exceed $1.5M` [Enter]

[Shift] + [Tab] `New Hires` [Enter]

[Tab] `Jamal Lawrence - Web Master` [Enter]

`Malika Fayza - Search Engine Specialist` [Enter]

`Jin Chen - Marketing Analyst` [Enter]

[Shift] + [Tab] `Thank You!` [Enter]

[Tab] `Our Success Is Your Success`

Your outline should match the following figure.

- ⊕ **iJams Music Distribution**
  - ⊖ A Year of Success
- ⊕ **Online Downloads**
  - ⊖ MP3 sales exceed $1M
  - ⊖ 350 thousand new user accounts
- ⊕ **Promotional Items**
  - ⊖ T-shirt sales exceed $500k
  - ⊖ Total promotional item sales exceed $1.5M
- ⊕ **New Hires**
  - ⊖ Jamal Lawrence – Web Master
  - ⊖ Malika Fayza – Search Engine Specialist
  - ⊖ Jin Chen – Marketing Analyst
- ⊕ **Thank You!**
  - ⊖ Our Success Is Your Success

8. Choose **File→Save As** and save the outline to the Lesson 02 folder as `iJams 2010`.

9. Choose **File→Exit** to close the outline and Word.
   Word closes and PowerPoint is visible.

Import the Outline

10. If necessary, **restore** PowerPoint from the Taskbar or start it if it is not running.

11. Choose **File→New** and double-click the **Blank Presentation** icon to create a new blank presentation.

12. Choose **Design→Themes→More→**▾**→Apothecary** from the Ribbon to apply a document theme.

13. Choose **Home→Slides→New Slide ▾ menu→Slides From Outline** from the Ribbon.

14. Use the **Insert Outline** dialog box to navigate to the Lesson 02 folder.

15. **Choose** the iJams 2010 outline and click the **Insert** button.
    PowerPoint will take a moment to import the outline. Note that the first slide is blank because Power-Point inserted the slides from the outline after the existing blank title slide.

16. Display the **Outline** tab on the Slides panel and examine the PowerPoint outline.
Observe that each Level 1 paragraph from the outline has become a slide title and each Level 2 paragraph has become a bulleted paragraph under the appropriate title.

17. Display the **Slides** tab to view the slide thumbnails.

18. **Choose** the first slide (the blank slide) and **tap** Delete to remove it.
The blank slide is deleted and the iJams Music Distribution slide becomes selected.

Change a Layout and Apply a Design Template

19. Choose **Home→Slides→Layout ▾menu→Title Slide** from the Ribbon.
The layout of the selected slide changes.

20. Select the final slide, Thank You, and choose **Home→Slides→Layout ▾menu→Section Header** from the Ribbon.

21. Choose the first slide, iJams Music Distribution.

Reset the Slide Formatting

22. Each slide is formatted with blue text because Word formatted the heading styles as blue. With the first slide selected, choose **Home→Slides→Reset**.
The text formatting is removed and returns to the default setting for the current document theme.

23. Select the second slide, **press** Shift, select the last slide, and **release** Shift.
Slides 2–5 become selected.

24. Choose **Home→Slides→Reset** to reformat the text on the selected slides with the document theme formatting.

25. Choose **File→Save As** and save the presentation as **iJams 2010** in the Lesson 02 folder.

2.4 Formatting Your Presentation

Video Lesson   labyrinthelab.com/videos

PowerPoint 2010 makes it so easy to create a presentation that the slides you create may not need any additional formatting. After all, the placeholders arrange the text, the bullets are automatic, and the color scheme is preformatted. However, in most cases, you will want to fine-tune your presentation. Formatting your presentation will make a good presentation even better.

Formatting Text

FROM THE KEYBOARD

Ctrl + B for bold
Ctrl + U for underline
Ctrl + I for italic

Formatting text is a common step in the development of a presentation. For instance, when reviewing a slide, you might decide that the text could be emphasized by changing the color of the font. If you had the time, you could change the font color of each piece of text on the slide individually by using the Font group on the Home tab of the Ribbon. However, a more efficient way to change the font color is to first select the placeholder and then apply the change of color. By selecting the placeholder, all text within the placeholder is changed in one swoop. The following illustration describes the buttons on the Home tab's Font group that assist you in formatting text.

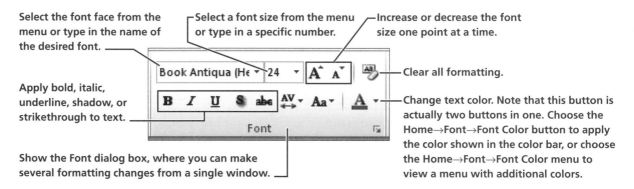

Select the font face from the menu or type in the name of the desired font.

Select a font size from the menu or type in a specific number.

Increase or decrease the font size one point at a time.

Clear all formatting.

Apply bold, italic, underline, shadow, or strikethrough to text.

Change text color. Note that this button is actually two buttons in one. Choose the Home→Font→Font Color button to apply the color shown in the color bar, or choose the Home→Font→Font Color menu to view a menu with additional colors.

Show the Font dialog box, where you can make several formatting changes from a single window.

Setting Character Spacing

Character spacing refers to the horizontal space between characters. PowerPoint lets you adjust this spacing to give your text some breathing room. If none of the preset options fit your needs, you can enter a numerical value to specify the exact amount of spacing. In the professional world of print, this is referred to as *tracking* or *kerning*. After selecting the characters you wish to space, choose the Home→ Font→Character Spacing button from the Ribbon to set your character spacing.

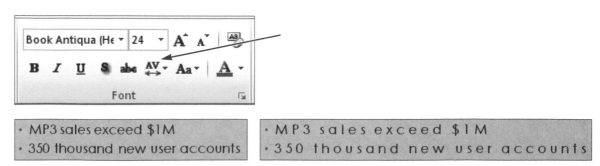

The same slide with no character spacing (left) and a large amount of character spacing applied (right)

Setting the Text Case

You can change the case of your text by selecting the text on your slide and choosing Home→ Font→Change Case from the Ribbon.

The following table illustrates the different options available with the Change Case button.

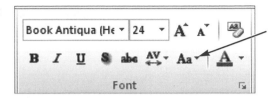

QUICK REFERENCE	SETTING THE TEXT CASE
Menu Option	**How It Affects Text**
Sentence Case	Your text will look like this.
Lowercase	your text will look like this.
Uppercase	YOUR TEXT WILL LOOK LIKE THIS.
Capitalize Each Word	Your Text Will Look Like This.
Toggle Case	Your text case will be toggled. Wherever you typed an uppercase letter, it will become lowercase. Wherever you typed a lowercase letter, it will become uppercase. *Example:* If you type **Your Text Will Look Like This**, Toggle Case will change it to **yOUR tEXT wILL lOOK lIKE tHIS**.

DEVELOP YOUR SKILLS 2.4.1
Format Text

In this exercise, you will change the formatting of the fonts in the Title and Subtitle slides.

Format the Subtitle

1. Follow these steps to display the Slides panel and display the title slide:

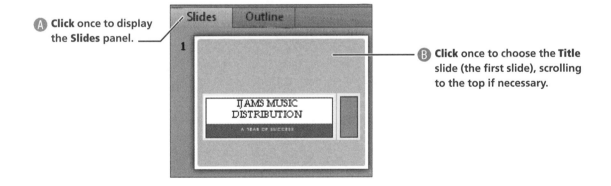

Ⓐ **Click** once to display the **Slides** panel.

Ⓑ **Click** once to choose the **Title** slide (the first slide), scrolling to the top if necessary.

2. Follow these steps to select the subtitle placeholder box:

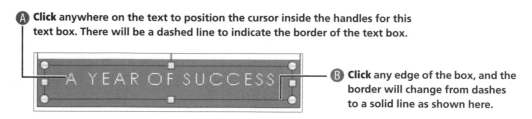

Ⓐ **Click** anywhere on the text to position the cursor inside the handles for this text box. There will be a dashed line to indicate the border of the text box.

Ⓑ **Click** any edge of the box, and the border will change from dashes to a solid line as shown here.

The solid line indicates that the text box is selected. Any formatting change you make now will affect all text within the box.

Notice also that the Home→Font→Font Size 18 ▾ *box on the Ribbon is currently set to 18. The Apothecary theme applied this font size to the subtitle.*

3. Choose **Home→Font→Decrease Font Size** A˅ from the Ribbon to reduce the font size to 16.

4. Choose **Home→Font→Bold** B from the Ribbon.
   PowerPoint makes the text bold.

5. Choose **Home→Font→Shadow** S from the Ribbon.
   The text stands out from the page a bit more because there is now a slight drop-shadow effect.

Format the Title

6. **Click** on the text of the title, iJams Music Distribution, and then **click** once on the dashed line border to select the Title text box.
   The title was formatted as uppercase by the Apothecary theme. The border changes to a solid line to indicate it is selected.

7. Choose **Home→Font→Change Case→Capitalize Each Word** from the Ribbon.
   The case is changed, but Ijams needs to be fixed.

8. **Double-click** the word *Ijams*, type **iJams**, and **tap** ⎡Spacebar⎤ to fix the case.

9. **Click** the dashed border around the title again to select the title box.

10. Choose **Home→Font→Font Size** ▾ from the Ribbon and point to several different font sizes.
    Notice how Live Preview displays the slide title size changes as you point to different settings on the Font Size menu.

11. Set the font size to **72**.
    The text is now too large and no longer fits nicely on the background.

12. **Click** on the 72 in the **Home→Font→Font Size** menu. Type **44** and **tap** ⎡Enter⎤.
    PowerPoint reduces the size of the text to 44. You can select a font size from the menu or type in your own value.

Setting Line Spacing

Video Lesson labyrinthelab.com/videos

Sometimes, instead of changing the font size or adding many hard returns, you need to only increase or decrease the spacing between lines to have the proper effect. *Line spacing* determines the amount of space between lines of text.

This setting is useful if text appears cramped and you wish to open up some breathing room between lines. Choose Home→Paragraph→Line Spacing to make your adjustments.

The same slide before and after applying Line Spacing

DEVELOP YOUR SKILLS 2.4.2
Adjust the Line Spacing

In this exercise, you will adjust the paragraph spacing to increase the amount of space between the bullets.

1. Display the **New Hires** slide on the Slides tab.

2. **Click** in any of the names to display a dashed border.

3. **Click** the dashed border to select the entire text box.

4. Choose **Home→Paragraph→Line Spacing** ⬍≣→**2.0** from the Ribbon to increase the spacing.
   PowerPoint redistributes the bulleted text vertically on the slide with more spacing between items.

5. **Save** 🖫 and **close** your presentation.

Setting Paragraph Alignment

Video Lesson labyrinthelab.com/videos

In time, you will be able to "eye" a presentation and notice if the paragraph alignment is not balanced. You can select one or more paragraphs and then click an alignment button on the Ribbon to make the change. Use the following buttons from the Home→Paragraph group on the Ribbon to realign paragraphs.

Purpose	Button	Example
Left-align	☰	This text has been left aligned. Notice how the left column is in a straight line, but the right column appears jagged.
Center-align	☰	This text has been center aligned. Notice how the text is balanced and centered.
Right-align	☰	This text has been right aligned. Notice how the right column is in a straight line.
Justify	☰	This text has been justify aligned. Notice how the text is spaced to maintain straight lines on the left and right.

DEVELOP YOUR SKILLS 2.4.3
Format the Contact Us Slide

In this exercise, you will reformat the Contact Us slide.

Format the Contact Us Slide

1. **Open** the iJams Contact presentation from your Lesson 02 folder.

2. If necessary, **display** the Slides panel.

3. If necessary, **scroll down** and then **select** Slide 5, Contact Us.

4. **Click** in the bulleted list and then **click** a border of the text box.

5. Choose **Home→Paragraph→Bullets** ≔ from the Ribbon to remove bullets from the paragraphs.

6. Choose **Home→Paragraph→Center** ☰ to center the paragraphs within the text box.

7. Drag to select the entire telephone number.
   A faded formatting box appears. Pointing your mouse at it will cause it to become more visible. You may format the selected text from this formatting box, but we will use the Ribbon as in the next steps.

8. Choose **Home→Font→Font Size** ▾ and increase the size to 32.

9. Using the same method, **increase** the size of the last line (the email address) to 32.

10. **Save** 🖫 your presentation.

2.5 Using the Format Painter

Video Lesson   labyrinthelab.com/videos

Common to all Office programs, the Format Painter is a great tool that simplifies the formatting process. The Format Painter copies all text formats including the typeface, size, color, and attributes such as bold, italic, and underline. It also copies formatting applied to shapes or clip art. The Format Painter helps you easily maintain a standardized, uniform look in your presentation.

Loading the Format Painter

The key to using the Format Painter successfully is understanding when it is loaded. After formatting has been copied with the Format Painter, its Ribbon icon appears pressed in. This pressed-in icon indicates that the Format painter is loaded and ready to use.

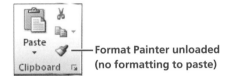 —Format Painter unloaded (no formatting to paste)    —Format Painter loaded and ready to paste formatting

QUICK REFERENCE	COPYING FORMATS WITH THE FORMAT PAINTER
Task	**Procedure**
Copy formats with the Format Painter	■ Select the object (text, picture, drawn line, etc.) with the format you wish to copy.
	■ Choose Home→Clipboard→Format Painter 🖌 from the Ribbon.
	■ Select the object at the new location to which you wish to copy formatting.
Use the Format Painter repeatedly	■ Select the object with formatting to be copied.
	■ Double-click Home→Clipboard→Format Painter 🖌 on the Ribbon.
	■ Click with the Format Painter on all objects to which you wish the formatting copied. (The Format Painter will remain active until you switch it off.)
	■ Click once on the Format Painter to switch it off again, or tap the [Esc] key.

 While using Format Painter, the mouse pointer changes from an arrow ☊ to a brush 🖌.

Copy Formatting with the Format Painter

In this exercise, you will copy and paste text formatting with the Format Painter.

Copy Text Formatting

1. Select the fourth slide, **New Artist Specials**.

2. **Double-click** *free* in the second bullet to select it.

3. Choose **Home→Font→Font Size→32** from the Ribbon.

4. Choose **Home→Font→Text Shadow** $\boxed{S}$ from the Ribbon.

5. Choose **Home→Font→Font Color ▾→Theme Colors→Red Accent 6** from the Ribbon.

6. Choose **Home→Clipboard→Format Painter** 🖌 from the Ribbon.
   The Format Painter icon is pressed in and is now loaded.

7. **Click** once on *July* in the last bullet.
   The formatting is copied to the word July, *and the Format Painter icon on the Ribbon becomes unloaded.*

8. Choose **Home→Clipboard→Format Painter** 🖌 from the Ribbon.
   The Format Painter has been reloaded with the formatting from the word July because that is where the insertion point is.

9. **Click** once on *20* in the last bullet.
   The formatting is copied to 20 *and the Format Painter on the Ribbon becomes unloaded.*

Use the Format Painter Repeatedly

10. Select the third slide, **Our Services**.

11. **Drag** across *on demand* in the first bullet to select it.

12. Choose **Home→Font→Bold** $\boxed{B}$ from the Ribbon.

13. Choose **Home→Font→Italic** $\boxed{I}$ from the Ribbon.

14. Choose **Home→Font→Font Color ▾→Theme Colors→Red Accent 6** from the Ribbon.

15. Double-click **Home→Clipboard→Format Painter** 🖌 on the Ribbon.
    Double-clicking the Format Painter will keep it loaded until you turn it off.

16. **Click** on the word *online* in the third bullet.
    The formatting is copied to online, *and the Format Painter remains loaded.*

17. **Click** on the word *sales* in the third bullet.

18. **Click** on the words *MP3* and *distribution* in the last bullet.

19. Choose **Home→Clipboard→Format Painter** 🖌 from the Ribbon.
    The Format Painter has been unloaded.

20. **Save** 🖫 your presentation.

2.6 Using the Slide Sorter

Video Lesson labyrinthelab.com/videos

Up until now, you've been working in the Normal view, which is good for manipulating a handful of slides. However, as your presentation grows to more slides than are visible in the Normal view, you will want to explore the function of the Slide Sorter view.

Rearranging Slides

PowerPoint's Slide Sorter view is used to rearrange slides. In the Slide Sorter view, each slide is a thumbnail image so the entire presentation is visible at a glance. As your presentation grows, often the order of the slides needs to be changed to create a logical concept flow. Using the Drag and Drop method in the Slide Sorter view, you can quickly reorganize your slides by moving them to the correct spot.

DEVELOP YOUR SKILLS 2.6.1
Use the Slide Sorter View

In this exercise, you will practice using the Slide Sorter view.

1. Choose **View→Presentation Views→Slide Sorter** 🔳 from the Ribbon.

2. Follow these steps to move a slide:

Ⓐ If necessary, use the Zoom slider in the bottom-right corner of your PowerPoint window to change the zoom percentage until all six slides are shown. Don't be concerned if your slides have a different arrangement than shown in the illustration.

Ⓑ **Drag** the Our Services slide to the left of the Packaging Options slide, and a large vertical bar will indicate the eventual position of the slide. Don't be concerned if your slides are on different rows or columns than shown here. Pay attention to the slide numbers, not the position on the grid.

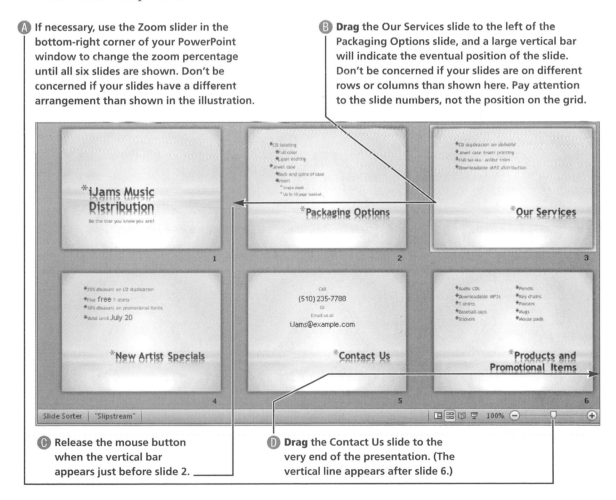

Ⓒ **Release** the mouse button when the vertical bar appears just before slide 2.

Ⓓ **Drag** the Contact Us slide to the very end of the presentation. (The vertical line appears after slide 6.)

3. Choose **Views→Presentation Views→Normal** ⊞ from the Ribbon to return to Normal view.

4. **Save** and **close** the presentation.

2.7 Organizing with Sections

Video Lesson   labyrinthelab.com/videos

Using the Slide Sorter with individual slides works well for small presentations. For presentations containing many slides, PowerPoint 2010's new Sections feature helps you keep them organized.

Creating Sections

Sections are always created before the selected slide and include all following slides. This often results in a section containing more slides than intended. The fix is to simply create another section after the intended last slide

QUICK REFERENCE	USING SECTIONS
Task	**Procedure**
Create a section	■ Select the first slide from the Slides panel for the section.
	■ Choose Home→Slides→Section→Add Section. A new section is started and includes all subsequent slides.
	■ Select the slide after the last slide in the section and choose Home→Slides→Section→Add Section. Section breaks are always created above the selected slide.
Name a section	■ Right-click the section's title bar and choose Rename Section.
	■ Type the new name for the section and click Rename.
Move a section	■ Drag a section's title bar above or below another section title bar.
Collapse or expand a section	■ Double-click the section's title bar.
Remove a section	■ Right-click the section's title bar and choose Remove Section to remove the section but leave the slides, or choose Remove Section & Slides to delete the section and its slides.

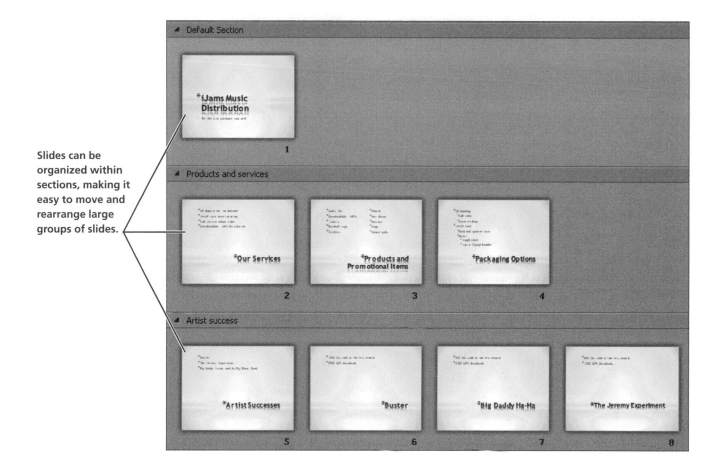

Slides can be organized within sections, making it easy to move and rearrange large groups of slides.

Create Sections

In this exercise, you will create sections.

1. **Open** the iJams Sections presentation from your Lesson 02 folder.
   With so many slides, it may be easier to work in Slide Sorter view.

2. Choose **View→Presentation Views→Slide Sorter** from the Ribbon.

3. Select slide 2, **Artist Successes**, and then choose **Home→Slides→Section→Add Section**.
   A new section named Untitled Section is created before the selected slide. Every slide below it is included in the section.

4. **Right-click** the section title bar and choose **Rename Section**, as in the figure to the right.

5. Type **Artist success** and click **Rename**.
   The section is renamed, but contains slides not intended for this section.

6. Select slide 6, **Our Services**, and then choose **Home→Slides→Section→Add Section**.
   A new section is started before the selected slide.

7. **Right-click** the Untitled Section title bar, choose **Rename Section**, and rename the section to `Products and services`.

8. **Click** the last slide, Contact Us, and **create** a new section before it.

9. **Rename** the final section `Call to action`.

10. **Save** your presentation.

Managing Sections

Video Lesson	labyrinthelab.com/videos

Once sections have been created, they can be dragged and rearranged in either the Slides panel or Slide Sorter view. Individual slides can even be dragged from one section to another. Additionally, sections can be collapsed similar to slide titles in Outline view. Collapsed sections hide the slides, making it easy to drag and reorder the sections. However, the collapsed sections only hide slides when editing. The collapsed slides will display as normal when running the slide show.

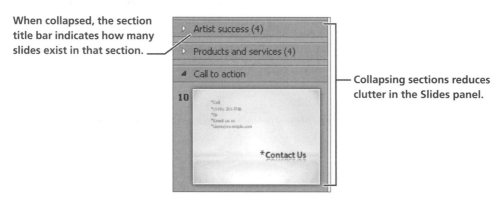

When collapsed, the section title bar indicates how many slides exist in that section.

Collapsing sections reduces clutter in the Slides panel.

DEVELOP YOUR SKILLS 2.7.2
Manage Sections

In this exercise, you will rearrange slides by using sections.

1. With the presentation still open in Slide Sorter view, **scroll** until you can see the Artist Success section title bar, if necessary.

2. **Double-click** the Artist Success section title bar to collapse it.

3. **Double-click** the Products and Services section title bar to collapse it.

4. Choose **View→Presentation Views→Normal** to switch to Normal view.
   The selected section does not remain collapsed when you change views.

5. **Double-click** the Products and services section title bar in the Slides panel to collapse it again.

6. Follow these steps to rearrange the sections:

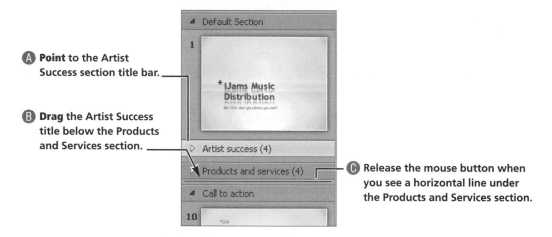

(A) **Point** to the Artist Success section title bar.

(B) **Drag** the Artist Success title below the Products and Services section.

(C) Release the mouse button when you see a horizontal line under the Products and Services section.

7. Choose **View→Presentation Views→Slide Sorter**.

8. **Double-click** the Products and Services section title bar to expand it.

9. **Click** anywhere in the gray area outside the slide thumbnails to deselect any slides.

10. **Scroll down**, if necessary, until you see the entire Call to Action section with the Contact Us slide.

11. Use the **Zoom slider** at the bottom-right corner of the PowerPoint window, if necessary, to make the view smaller. You should see all slides in both the Products and Services and Call to Action sections.

12. **Drag** the last slide of the Products and Services section (New Artist Specials) to the left of the Contact Us slide to move it to the Call to Action section. The Call to Action section should resemble the following figure.

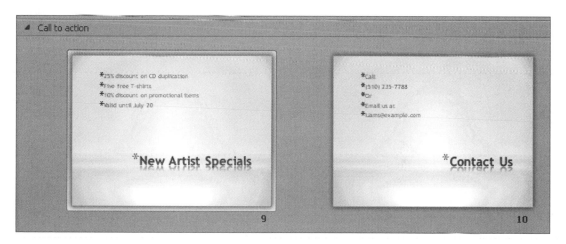

13. **Save** your presentation.

2.8 Printing Your Presentation

Video Lesson labyrinthelab.com/videos

Ninety percent of the time, you will be viewing or projecting the presentations you create from a PC or notebook computer. However, there may be times when a hard copy of the presentation is needed. In this lesson, you will simply explore the options of printing a presentation. In future lessons, you will apply this knowledge to printing handout slides and speaker notes as well.

Knowing What You Can Print

PowerPoint can create the following types of printouts:

- Slides: Prints each slide of a presentation on a separate page
- Handouts: Prints one or more slides per page, leaving room for attendees to jot notes during the presentation
- Speaker Notes: Prints each slide on a separate page, with any speaker notes you created for the slide below
- Outline: Prints a text outline of each slide, similar to what is seen in the Outline panel

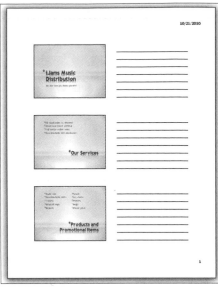

An example of a handout with three slides per page

Previewing a Printout

FROM THE KEYBOARD

Ctrl + P to display the Print tab in Backstage view

The Print window lets you see how each slide will be printed. You can then refine the appearance before printing. The following illustration describes the options available from the Print window.

The Print tab is available from Backstage view.

Choose to print all slides, a range of slides, or specific sections.

Choose the layout, such as the number of slides per page, lines for note taking, or text outline.

The Printer section allows you to choose a printer.

This button sends the print job to the printer.

You can specify the number of copies to be printed.

Choose how to print multipage presentations.

Print in color, grayscale, or black and white.

A preview of what will be printed appears here.

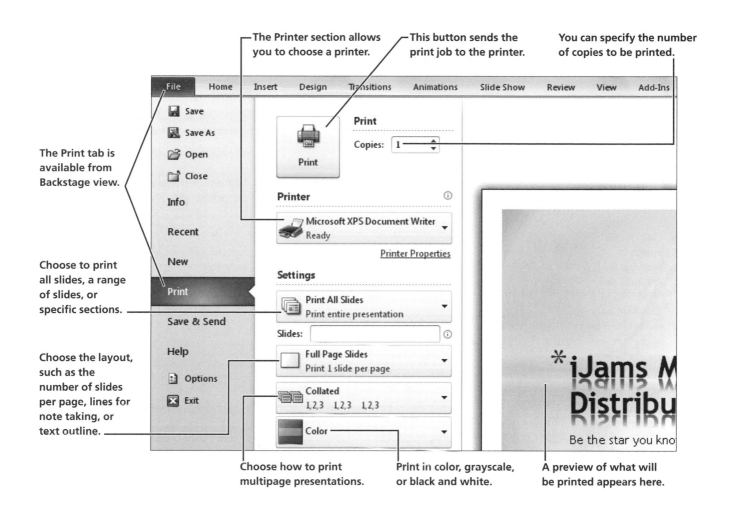

Preview a Printout

In this exercise, you will use Backstage view to preview a printout.

1. Choose **File→Print**.

2. Follow these steps to examine the print options:

Ⓐ Notice all ten slides in the presentation are set to be printed. Use the **left arrow** to return to the first slide. You can also use the scrollbar to navigate among slides.

Ⓑ Adjust the **Zoom** level so the whole slide fits in the preview.

Ⓒ Change this option to **Sections→ Products and Services** and note that only the three slides in that section are set to print.

Ⓓ Change this option to **Handouts→ 3 Slides** to preview the text outline. Changing this option to anything other than Full Page Slides causes the Orientation option to appear between the Collated and Color options.

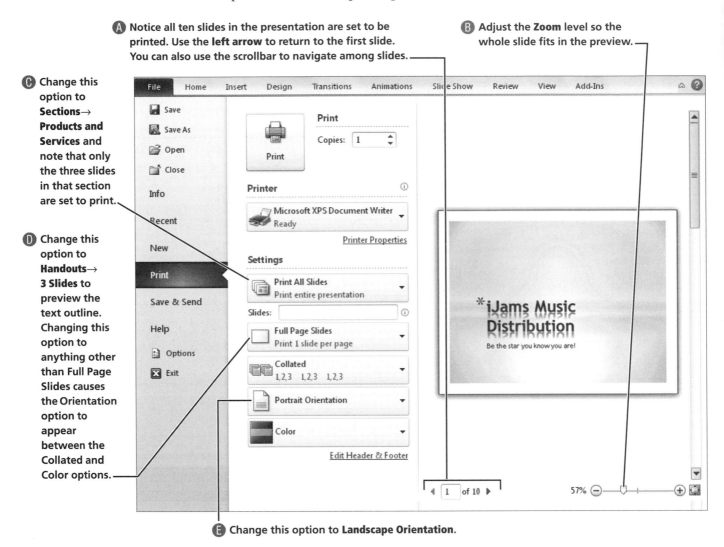

Ⓔ Change this option to **Landscape Orientation**.

3. Choose the **Home** tab from the Ribbon to exit Backstage view without printing.

Using Page Setup and Output Formats

Video Lesson labyrinthelab.com/videos

If you need to print the presentation itself or transparencies for overhead projection, use the Page Setup dialog box. The Page Setup dialog box can be displayed by choosing Design→Page Setup→Page Setup from the Ribbon. Examine the Page Setup options, along with the different types of output formats you can use by studying the Page Setup dialog box that follows:

PowerPoint provides a variety of output formats in the Slides Sized For menu. Available sizes include overhead transparencies, letter paper, banner, and other various sizes.

PowerPoint sets the size options depending on the output format. However, you can always manually adjust the size.

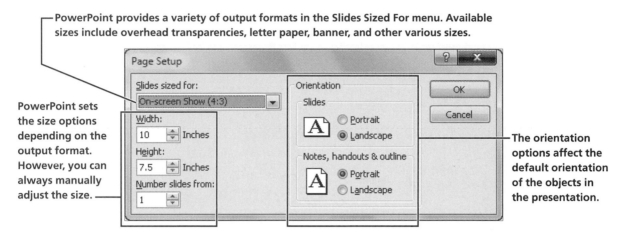

The orientation options affect the default orientation of the objects in the presentation.

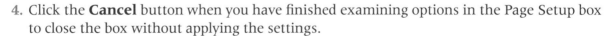

DEVELOP YOUR SKILLS 2.8.2
Explore the Page Setup Box

In this exercise, you will learn about the options provided in the Page Setup dialog box.

1. Choose **Design→Page Setup→Page Setup** as shown at right to display the Page Setup dialog box.

2. Click the **Slides Sized For** list and examine the various output formats.

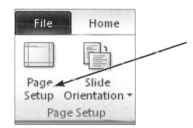

3. Examine the **Orientation** section of the Page Setup dialog box.
   Notice that there are separate settings for printing slides and printing notes and handout pages.

4. Click the **Cancel** button when you have finished examining options in the Page Setup box to close the box without applying the settings.

5. Choose **File→Close** from the Ribbon to close the presentation. Choose **Don't Save** if asked to save your changes.

Using the Print Shortcut

If you have customized your Quick Access toolbar to display the Quick Print icon, you may find it tempting to just click the Quick Print button. However, before this becomes a habit, know that a click of this button sends the entire presentation to the current printer, whether or not you want to make adjustments. If you are working with a document theme that has a colored background, the printing process will not only be painstakingly slow, but may also waste your toner or ink!

2.9 Concepts Review

Concepts Review labyrinthelab.com/pp10

To check your knowledge of the key concepts introduced in this lesson, complete the Concepts Review quiz by going to the URL listed above. If your classroom is using Labyrinth eLab, you may complete the Concepts Review quiz from within your eLab course.

Reinforce Your Skills

Practice Formatting

In this exercise, you will format some slides in the Tropical Getaways presentation.

1. Format the Presentation

2. **Open** the rs-Tropical Getaways Design presentation from the Lesson 02 folder.

3. Choose **View→Presentation Views→Normal** from the Ribbon and **select** the title slide from the Slides panel.

4. Click the **Title** box, and then **click** again on the edge of the box to select it.

5. Choose **Home→Font→Increase Font Size** from the Ribbon once to increase the font size.

6. Choose **Home→Font→Bold** to make the title bold.

Change Paragraph Alignment

7. **Display** the Travel Now And Save! slide on the Slides panel.

8. Choose **Home→Slides→New Slide** to add a new slide after Travel Now And Save!

9. Type **Travel Categories** for the title.

10. **Type** the following as bulleted paragraphs:
    - **Adventure**
    - **Leisure**
    - **Family**
    - **Singles**

11. Select the **bulleted text box** by clicking on the border.

12. Choose the **Home→Paragraph→Bullets** button from the Ribbon to remove the bullets from all paragraphs.

13. Choose the **Home→Paragraph→Center** button from the Ribbon to center the text on the slide.

14. Choose **Home→Paragraph→Line Spacing→2.0** to increase the vertical spacing between the bullets.
    After you finish, the slide should appear like the following illustration.

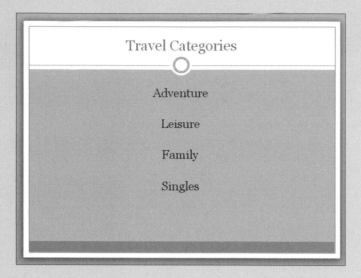

15. Save the presentation and continue with the next exercise.

Rearrange Sections

In this exercise, you will create and rearrange sections.

Before you begin: The rs-Tropical Getaways Design presentation in the Lesson 02 folder should be open.

1. Choose **View→Presentation Views→Slide Sorter** from the Ribbon.

2. Select the **Complete Packages** slide.

3. Choose **Home→Slides→Section→Add Section**.

4. **Right-click** the Untitled Section title bar and **choose** Rename Section.

5. Type **Prices** and click Rename.

6. Select the **Travel Categories** slide and choose **Home→Slides→Section→Add Section**.

7. **Right-click** the Untitled Section title bar and **choose** Rename Section.

8. Type **Locations** and **click** Rename.

9. **Select** the Contact Us slide and create a section named **Contact**.

10. **Right-click** the Contact section and **choose** Collapse All.

11. **Drag** the Locations section above the Prices section. Your screen should resemble the following figure.

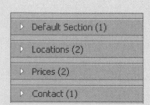

12. **Right-click** any of the sections and choose Expand All.

13. Choose **View→Presentation Views→Normal** from the Ribbon.

14. **Save** your presentation.

Print the Presentation

In this exercise, you will print a slide.

Before You Begin: The rs-Tropical Getaways presentation in the Lesson 02 folder should be open.

1. Select the second slide, **Travel Categories**, from the Slides panel.

2. Choose **File→Print** to display the Print tab in Backstage view.

3. Follow these steps to set the print options:

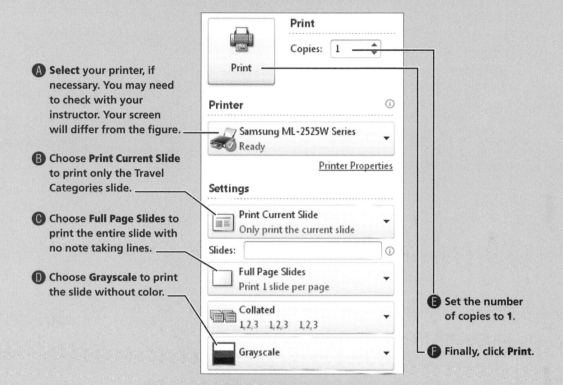

Ⓐ **Select** your printer, if necessary. You may need to check with your instructor. Your screen will differ from the figure.

Ⓑ Choose **Print Current Slide** to print only the Travel Categories slide.

Ⓒ Choose **Full Page Slides** to print the entire slide with no note taking lines.

Ⓓ Choose **Grayscale** to print the slide without color.

Ⓔ Set the number of copies to **1**.

Ⓕ Finally, click **Print**.

4. **Save** and **close** the presentation.

Apply Your Skills

Reformat a Presentation

In this exercise, you will add a slide to the Classic Cars Design presentation and change the format.

1. **Open** the as-Classic Cars Design presentation from your Lesson 02 folder.

2. **Add** a new slide after the title slide and **type** the following text:

Title	Agenda for 2010 Convention
Bulleted Paragraphs	▪ Locating a Classic Car over the Internet
	▪ Negotiating the Price
	▪ Resources for Restoring
	▪ The 10 Most Popular Road Trips
	▪ Displaying Your Classic Car
	▪ Joining a Classic Car Club
	▪ Insuring your Classic Car
	▪ Leadership Elections

3. Apply the **Two Content** layout to the slide.

4. Move the last four bullets into the **right column**.

5. Increase the **line spacing** of both bulleted lists to **1.5**.

6. Apply a **font size** of **22** to both bulleted lists.
   Your slide should look similar to the following illustration:

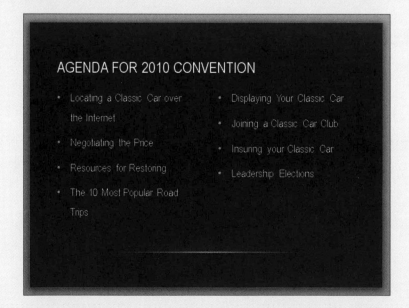

7. **Save** your presentation.

Print a Slide

In this exercise, you will print a slide.

Before You Begin: You must have completed Apply Your Skills 2.1 before you can begin this exercise.

1. If necessary, **open** the as-Classic Cars Design presentation from the Lesson 02 folder.

2. Select the **Agenda for 2010 Convention** slide.

3. Using the Grayscale option, **print** the single slide.

4. **Save** the changes to the as-Classic Cars Design presentation.

5. **Close** the presentation.

Critical Thinking & Work-Readiness Skills

In the course of working through the following Microsoft Office-based Critical Thinking exercises, you will also be utilizing various work-readiness skills, some of which are listed next to each exercise. Go to labyrinthelab.com/ workreadiness *to learn more about the work-readiness skills.*

2.1 Use the Outline Panel and Repurpose a Presentation

WORK-READINESS SKILLS APPLIED

- Reading
- Reasoning
- Organizing and maintaining information

Aurelia, the administrative assistant, has been tasked by Carthic to take the presentation he used at JamWorks and polish it into a general presentation he and others can give to any group interested in learning what iJams is all about. Open ct-JamWorks from your Lesson 02 folder and, using the Outline Panel, identify and delete any slides that were only appropriate for the JamWorks conference. Use the Outline panel to add any additional slides you think are necessary. Save the presentation as **ct-JamWorks Revised** to your Lesson 02 folder.

2.2 Format a Presentation

WORK-READINESS SKILLS APPLIED

- Thinking
- Organizing and maintaining information
- Seeing things in the mind's eye

Start with the ct-JamWorks Revised presentation you created in the previous exercise and save it to your Lesson 02 folder with the new name **ct-JamWorks Formatted**. View it as a slide show and ask yourself if the slides are easy to read and in the best order. Change the document theme, adjust the text layout, rearrange the order of slides, and make any other changes you feel are necessary. Use the Format Painter to quickly duplicate formatting changes. Save your changes.

2.3 Print a Presentation

WORK-READINESS SKILLS APPLIED

- Serving clients/ customers
- Reasoning
- Writing

Presenters often like to review their presentations in print (though some are happy to review and comment in digital format). Carthic likes to edit on paper, so Aurelia wants to give the new general presentation to him in a form he feels comfortable with. Open the ct-JamWorks Formatted presentation, if necessary. Use various tools to check for a final time that the content is as you wish it. Use the Print Preview feature as you test various print options. Then, print the slides, deciding which view would be best and easiest for Carthic's review. Type and print a brief Word memo to accompany the printed slides.

Adding Graphics,
Animation, and Sound

LEARNING OBJECTIVES

After studying this lesson, you will be able to:

- Add clip art, photos, and screen shots to a presentation
- Remove backgrounds and apply artistic effects to slide images
- Add transition effects to a slide show
- Add animation to objects on a slide
- Add sound effects to transitions and animations

In this lesson, you will enhance the iJams presentation that you created in previous lessons. You will use clip art to add interest to the presentation, a drawing object to add spark, and slide transitions and animation to "bring the presentation to life."

Adding Eye Candy

The iJams presentation is evolving nicely. However, Carthic Maddix returns from the JamWorks trade show knowing he will have to add some pizzazz to the presentation if he is to compete with his competitors. Although Carthic and Aurelia have created an error-free, technically perfect presentation, he can see that something is definitely missing! Aurelia suggests sprinkling clip art to illustrate Carthic's message. Knowing the robust animation tools in PowerPoint 2010, she also encourages Carthic to consider using animation to give life to the presentation. They decide that if used sparingly, clip art and animation will enhance their presentation.

The iJams presentation with stock clip art added

3.1 Working with Clip Art

Video Lesson   labyrinthelab.com/videos

Adding clip art to your presentations will help you emphasize key points and add polish to the presentation as a whole. Microsoft Office 2010 has a clip art collection of more than 130,000 pieces of art—and it grows daily. There is clip art available for any occasion.

Using Text and Object Layouts

PowerPoint creates slides with different layouts, such as slides with titles only and slides with titles and text. These slide layouts allow you to easily create slides with a standardized title and bulleted text. Many of PowerPoint's layouts, including the Title and Content layout and the Two Content layout, provide placeholders for titles, text, and various types of content including tables, charts, clip art, pictures, diagrams, organizational charts, and movies.

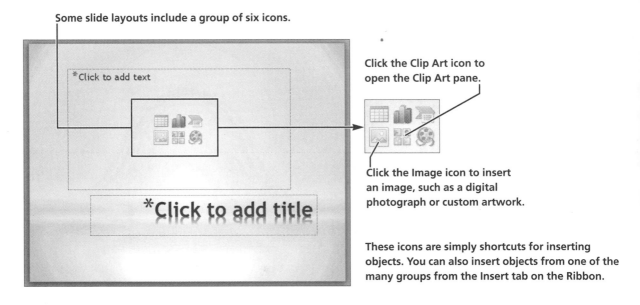

Some slide layouts include a group of six icons.

*Click to add text

*Click to add title

Click the Clip Art icon to open the Clip Art pane.

Click the Image icon to insert an image, such as a digital photograph or custom artwork.

These icons are simply shortcuts for inserting objects. You can also insert objects from one of the many groups from the Insert tab on the Ribbon.

QUICK REFERENCE	WORKING WITH SLIDE INSERT SHORTCUTS		
Icon	**What It Does**	**Icon**	**What It Does**
	Inserts a table		Inserts an image
	Inserts a chart or graph		Inserts a SmartArt graphic
	Opens the Clip Art pane to insert clip art		Inserts a media clip

Deleting Placeholder Text

Sometimes you may decide to simply replace all the text on a slide with a graphic. Deleting all the text inside a placeholder results in the slide displaying its six default insert icons, making it easy to insert clip art or other objects.

When all the text inside a placeholder is deleted...

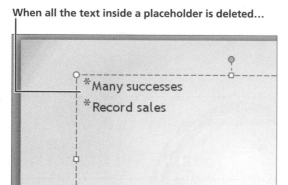

...the six insert icons reappear.

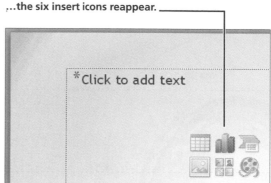

DEVELOP YOUR SKILLS 3.1.1

Get a Slide Ready for Clip Art

In this exercise, you will get a slide ready to accept clip art. The clip art will be added in the next exercise.

1. **Open** the iJams Animation presentation from the Lesson 03 folder on your file storage location.

2. If necessary, choose **View→Presentation Views→Normal** to display the presentation in **Normal** view.
   If it was not visible before, the Slides/Outline panel now appears on the left side of the PowerPoint window.

3. If necessary, choose the **Slides** tab in the Slides/Outline panel.
   It will be easier to monitor your slide layouts if you are using the Slides panel rather than the Outline panel.

4. Select the **Our Services** slide from the Slides panel.

5. Choose **Home→Slides→New Slide** .
   A new slide is inserted below Our Services. The new slide uses the same layout as the Our Services slide.

Choose a Layout and Format Text

6. Follow these steps to apply a slide layout suitable for clip art:

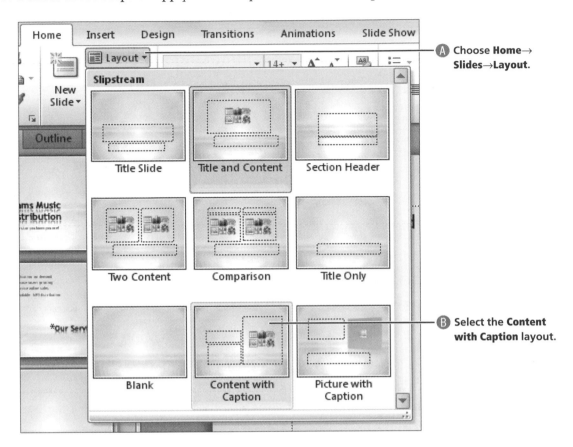

A Choose **Home→ Slides→Layout**.

B Select the **Content with Caption** layout.

7. In the Title placeholder, type **Our Recent Success**.

8. In the text box beneath the title, **type**

   Top of the Rock `Enter` **Excellence in Service to Musicians** `Enter` **League of Electronic Music Distributors.**

9. **Select** the text *Top of the Rock* and increase the font size to 24 from the **Home→Font→ Font Size menu ▼** button.

10. Choose **Home→Font→Bold** to make the text bold.

11. Select the text *League of Electronic Music Distributors.*

12. Choose **Home→Font→Italic** to make the text italic.
    Your slide is ready to have clip art added.

13. **Click** in the large text placeholder at the right and type **Many successes** `Enter` **Record breaking sales**.
    You decide instead to replace the bulleted text with clip art. You will delete all the text in the placeholder so the slide displays the six inert icons again.

14. Follow these steps to delete all the text in the placeholder:

(A) **Point** to the dashed border of the large text placeholder until your mouse pointer turns into a four-headed arrow and then **click** the dashed border to select the placeholder. The border turns solid to indicate the placeholder is selected.

(B) Tap [Delete]. The text, not the placeholder itself, is deleted and the six insert icons appear.

* Many successes
* Record breaking sales

15. **Save** 💾 your presentation.

Searching for Clip Art with the Clip Art Task Pane

Video Lesson   labyrinthelab.com/videos

Finding clip art is easy: Click the Clip Art 🖼 icon in the slide placeholder to bring the Clip Art task pane to the right side of your screen. Alternatively, you can select Insert→Images→Clip Art from the Ribbon. You search for clip art by typing a keyword and clicking the Go button. Each piece of clip art is associated with keywords that describe its characteristics. For example, the images shown in the illustration can be located by using the keyword *awards* or *prizes*. The following illustration describes the Clip Art task pane.

An image can be located by typing a keyword and clicking the Go button.

You can limit your search by searching only your computer or including the online Microsoft Clip Art gallery.

You can filter your results by searching for specific media types, such as clip art, photographs, movies, or sounds.

The scroll bar is used to browse the clip art images resulting from your search.

The desired image can be inserted by clicking it.

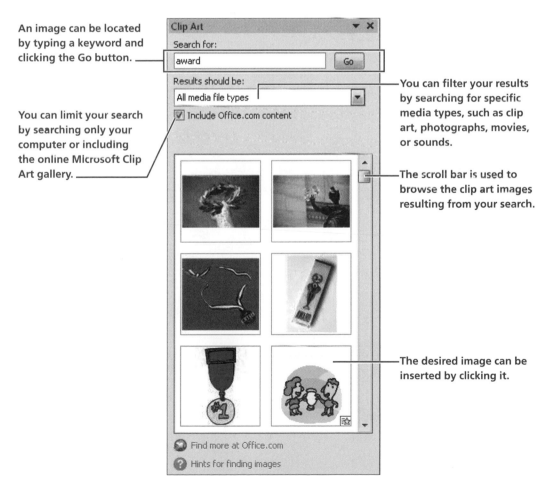

Insert Clip Art

In this exercise, you will insert clip art.

1. On the Our Recent Success slide, click the **Clip Art** icon as shown to open the Clip Art task pane.

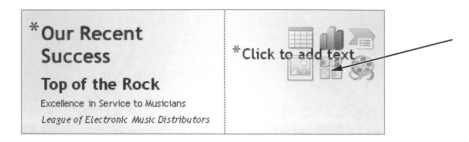

2. Configure the Clip Art task pane as shown:

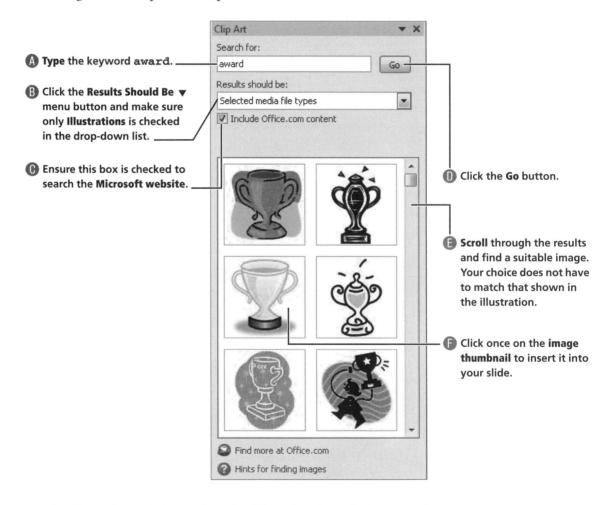

Ⓐ **Type** the keyword `award`.

Ⓑ Click the **Results Should Be ▼** menu button and make sure only **Illustrations** is checked in the drop-down list.

Ⓒ **Ensure** this box is checked to search the **Microsoft website.**

Ⓓ Click the **Go** button.

Ⓔ **Scroll** through the results and find a suitable image. Your choice does not have to match that shown in the illustration.

Ⓕ **Click** once on the **image thumbnail** to insert it into your slide.

The clip art image is inserted on the slide and replaces the large text box.

Moving, Sizing, and Rotating Objects

Video Lesson labyrinthelab.com/videos

When you click an object (such as a clip art image), sizing handles and a rotate handle appear. You can easily move, size, and rotate selected objects as described in the following illustration.

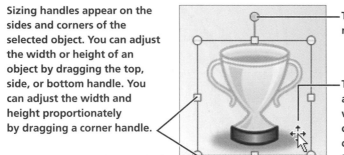

Sizing handles appear on the sides and corners of the selected object. You can adjust the width or height of an object by dragging the top, side, or bottom handle. You can adjust the width and height proportionately by dragging a corner handle.

The green rotate handle rotates the object.

The Move pointer appears as a four-headed arrow when you point to an object. You can move an object by dragging it while the Move pointer is visible.

DEVELOP YOUR SKILLS 3.1.3
Move and Size Clip Art

In this exercise, you will manipulate clip art, sizing and moving it to place it on the slide.

1. Follow these steps to rotate the clip art image:

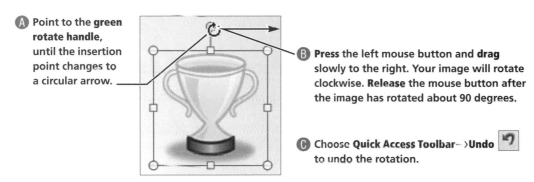

A Point to the **green rotate handle**, until the insertion point changes to a circular arrow.

B **Press** the left mouse button and **drag** slowly to the right. Your image will rotate clockwise. **Release** the mouse button after the image has rotated about 90 degrees.

C Choose **Quick Access Toolbar→Undo** to undo the rotation.

2. Follow these steps to resize the clip art image:

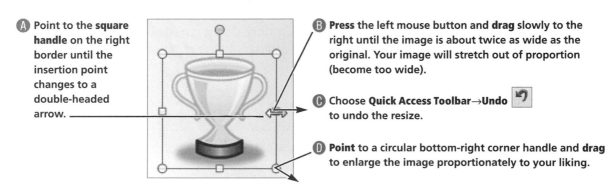

A Point to the **square handle** on the right border until the insertion point changes to a double-headed arrow.

B **Press** the left mouse button and **drag** slowly to the right until the image is about twice as wide as the original. Your image will stretch out of proportion (become too wide).

C Choose **Quick Access Toolbar→Undo** to undo the resize.

D **Point** to a circular bottom-right corner handle and **drag** to enlarge the image proportionately to your liking.

3. Point to the **image** itself (not the border or a resize handle) until the pointer becomes a four-headed arrow. **Drag** the image so it is centered next to the bar of text. Compare your slide with the following illustration.

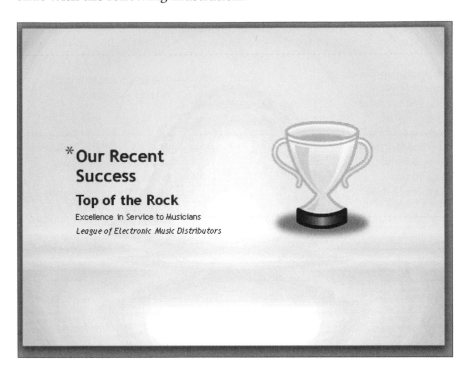

4. **Save** 💾 your presentation.

Inserting Clip Art Without an Existing Placeholder

Video Lesson labyrinthelab.com/videos

If your slide does not have the shortcut icons to insert clip art, you can still insert an image by displaying the Clip Art task pane and choosing Insert→Images→Clip Art from the Ribbon.

Formatting Clip Art

After your image is on the slide, use the various groups on the contextual Format tab to add effects or align your image. You can add borders, drop-shadows, or bevels, rotate your image in 3-D from the Format→Picture Styles group. Other groups on the Format tab allow you to align, flip, crop, or perform basic image editing tasks.

QUICK REFERENCE	PERFORMING CLIP ART TASKS
Task	**Procedure**
Insert a clip art image	■ Click the Clip Art shortcut on the slide to display the Clip Art task pane. ■ Enter a keyword and configure the Results Should Be and Include Office.com Content options. ■ Click the Go button. ■ Click the desired thumbnail to insert the clip art in your slide.
Resize a clip art image	■ Click the clip art image to display its border. ■ Drag any square handle along the top, bottom, or sides of the clip art's border to resize the image wider or taller. ■ Drag any circular handle in the clip art's corners to resize the image proportionately.
Move a clip art image	■ Point to the image until the mouse pointer becomes a four-headed arrow. ■ Drag the image to the desired location.
Rotate a clip art image	■ Click the clip art image to display its border. ■ Point to the green rotate handle on top of the clip art's border until the mouse pointer becomes a circular arrow. ■ Drag left or right to rotate the image.
Format a clip art image	■ Click the clip art image to display its border. ■ Select a command from the Format→Picture Styles group on the Ribbon.

DEVELOP YOUR SKILLS 3.1.4

Insert and Format Clip Art

In this exercise, you will work with the Ribbon to insert and format an image on your slide.

Insert the Image

1. Display the **title slide**.
2. Choose **Insert→Images→Clip Art** from the Ribbon if the Clip Art task pane is not already visible.
   The Clip Art task pane should be displayed on the right side of your screen.

3. Follow these steps to insert clip art on the title slide:

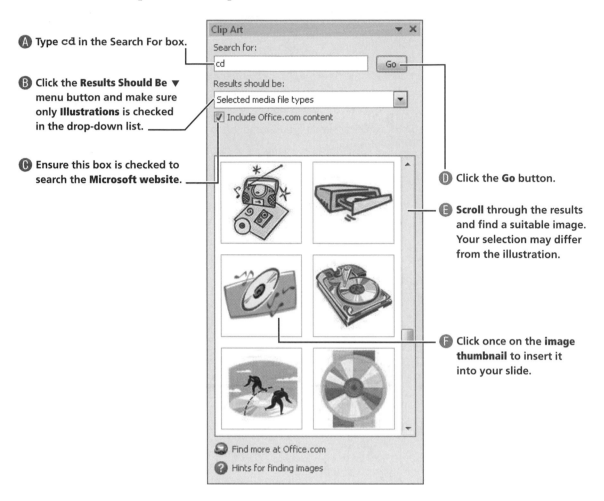

A Type **cd** in the Search For box.

B Click the **Results Should Be** ▼ menu button and make sure only **Illustrations** is checked in the drop-down list.

C Ensure this box is checked to search the **Microsoft website**.

D Click the **Go** button.

E **Scroll** through the results and find a suitable image. Your selection may differ from the illustration.

F Click once on the **image thumbnail** to insert it into your slide.

Size and Position the Image

In the next few steps, you will use the Format contextual tab to experiment with effect options.

4. Drag the image to the top of the slide so it no longer overlaps the text, and then **drag** the top-right circular handle toward the top-right corner of your slide to enlarge the image proportionately. Be careful not to size it too large. The image should still fit on the slide.

5. Choose **Format→Arrange→Align→Align Center** from the Ribbon to center the image horizontally.
Selecting an image object forces the display of the contextual Format tab.

6. Follow these steps to format the image:
   - Make sure the image displays handles to indicate it is selected.
   - Choose **Format→Picture Styles→Picture Effects** 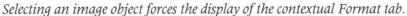 from the Ribbon.

7. **Roll** your insertion point over several of the items in the **Picture Effects** gallery to view a Live Preview of each effect.
As you have seen with other commands, Live Preview makes it easy to anticipate the effect of a command without the need to undo it if you don't like the effect.

8. Choose **Format→Picture Styles→Picture Effects** →**Glow**→**Turquoise, 18 pt glow, Accent color 2** as shown in the following illustration.

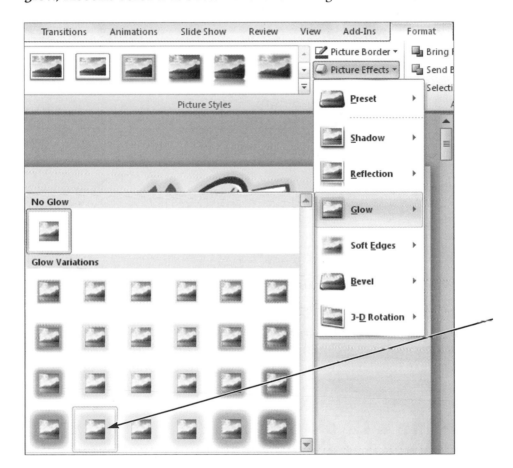

PowerPoint applies a glowing effect to the edge of the image.

9. **Close** the Clip Art task pane.

10. Compare your finished slide to the following illustration.

The completed title slide

11. Save your presentation.

3.2 Adding Other Graphics

Video Lesson   labyrinthelab.com/videos

Sometimes you just can't find that perfect image through clip art. Oftentimes you can incorporate more unique and personal imagery if you take your own pictures or download professional photographs from a commercial website. PowerPoint 2010 has some new tools and features to make the most of your images, including the ability to remove a background and add artistic effects.

Removing a Background

Many times a photograph contains more than what you need. In the past, it was necessary to learn how to use a graphics editing program to remove the background or other unwanted elements. PowerPoint 2010 includes a new feature that allows you to remove backgrounds with just a few clicks. When removing a background the original picture is not harmed, because PowerPoint works on a copy of the picture embedded into the slide. Additionally, nothing is actually removed from the picture. PowerPoint just hides areas of the picture you mark as those to be removed. The hidden areas can always be made visible again. You can adjust the settings of the removal tool at any time after the background's initial removal, so there is no need to worry about getting it perfect on your first try.

The Background Removal tool overlays in purple the areas to be removed.

With just a few clicks, the background can be removed.

Remove a Background

In this exercise, you will insert a picture and remove the background.

Insert a Picture

1. **Scroll down** the Slides pane, if necessary, and **select** the sixth slide, Artist Successes.

2. Choose **Insert→Images→Picture** from the Ribbon.

3. **Navigate** to your Lesson 03 folder, select the picture **Guitarist Back**, and click **Insert**.
   The picture is inserted on the slide, but contains more imagery than we need.

Remove the Background

4. **Drag** the picture up so the top of the picture snaps to the top of the slide.

5. **Drag** the bottom-left circular handle down and to the left until the bottom of the picture snaps to the bottom of the slide.
   The picture now covers the whole slide.

6. Choose **Picture Tools→Format→Adjust→Remove Background**.
   PowerPoint places a rectangle border inside the picture and does its best to guess what you want to remove. A purple overlay indicates what will be removed. You will adjust this.

7. **Drag** the top-right circular handle of the rectangular box inside the picture so it snaps to the top-right corner of the picture.

8. **Drag** the bottom-left circular handle of the rectangular box down and to the right so the entire guitar is inside the box. Your slide should resemble the following figure, but it will not be exact.

When you resize the box inside the picture, PowerPoint adjusts the purple overlay. The overlay still needs to be adjusted so we can see the whole guitarist.

9. Choose **Background Removal→Refine→Mark Areas to Keep**.

10. Follow these steps to adjust the overlay:

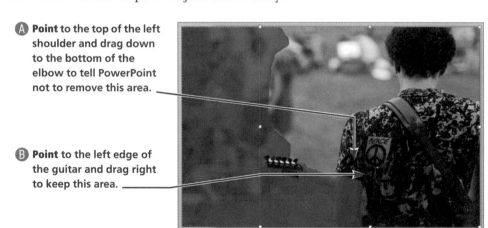

Ⓐ **Point** to the top of the left shoulder and drag down to the bottom of the elbow to tell PowerPoint not to remove this area.

Ⓑ **Point** to the left edge of the guitar and drag right to keep this area.

Ⓒ **Drag** over any other purple on the guitarist or the guitar.

11. Choose **Background Removal→Refine→Mark Areas to Remove**.

12. Follow these steps to define areas to be removed:

Ⓐ **Drag** over the background to tell PowerPoint to remove this area.

Ⓑ **Drag** over this section to remove it as well.

13. You will probably have to go back and forth with the Mark Areas to Keep and Mark Areas to Remove buttons as you continue to tweak the purple overlay. When done, your slide should match the following figure.

14. Choose **Background Removal→Close→Keep Changes**. Your slide should resemble the following figure. If it doesn't, choose **Picture Tools→Format→Adjust→Remove Background** to adjust the overlay.

15. Save your presentation.

Applying Artistic Effects

Video Lesson   labyrinthelab.com/videos

PowerPoint 2010 includes new artistic effects that can be applied to pictures, making photographs look like pencil sketches, cement, or pastels. Additionally, pictures can be re-colored to create a color cast that blends with your theme.

The picture before any effect has been applied

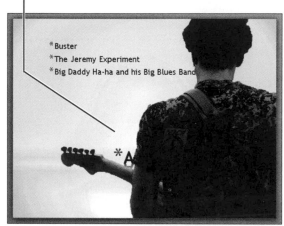

The picture after the Pencil Grayscale and recolor effects have been applied

QUICK REFERENCE	MODIFYING PICTURES
Task	**Procedure**
Insert a picture from your computer	■ Choose Insert→Images→Picture from the Ribbon. ■ Navigate your hard drive to the picture you want to use. ■ Select your picture and click Insert.
Remove a background	■ Select the picture and choose Picture Tools→Format→Adjust→Remove Background from the Ribbon. ■ Adjust the marquee to include the portion of the picture you want to keep. ■ To mark additional areas of the picture to include, choose Background Removal→Refine→Mark Areas to Keep and drag over the areas of the picture to keep. ■ To mark additional areas of the picture to exclude, choose Background Removal→Refine→Mark Areas to Remove and drag over the areas of the picture to exclude. ■ Choose Background Removal→Refine→Keep Changes to apply your settings. ■ Choose Picture Tools→Format→Adjust→Remove Background from the Ribbon to adjust the background removal at any time.
Apply artistic effects	■ Select the picture and choose Picture Tools→Format→Adjust→Artistic Effects from the Ribbon. ■ Choose an effect to apply the default settings, or choose Artistic Effects Options to customize the settings. ■ If you choose to customize the settings, choose an effect from the drop-down menu and adjust its settings and click Close.

Apply Artistic Effects

In this exercise, you will apply artistic effects to a picture.

1. If necessary, select the picture on the sixth slide, **Artistic Successes**.
   The picture is covering up the text. You will move it behind the text.

2. Choose **Picture Tools→Format→Arrange→Send Backward ▼→Send to Back** from the Ribbon.
   The picture appears behind the text, but is still too dark to see the text.

3. Choose **Picture Tools→Format→Adjust→Color** from the Ribbon.

4. Point to several **color adjustments** to see how they change the picture on the slide. Notice a tooltip appears when you point to an adjustment, indicating its name.

5. Select the **Recolor→Washout** adjustment to fade out the picture.

The text can now be seen, but the picture is a little too crisp and distracts from the text. You will blur it slightly to move it further into the background.

6. Choose **Picture Tools→Format→Adjust→Artistic Effects** from the Ribbon.

7. Point to several **effects** to see how they change the picture on the slide. Notice a tooltip appears when you point to an effect, indicating the name of the effect.

8. Point to the **Blur** effect, the last thumbnail in the second row, and see how it affects the picture.
   The default blur effect is too blurry.

9. Choose **Picture Tools→Format→Adjust→Artistic Effects→Artistic Effects Options** from the Ribbon.

10. Follow these steps to customize the Blur effect:

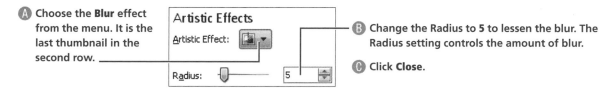

Ⓐ Choose the **Blur** effect from the menu. It is the last thumbnail in the second row.

Ⓑ Change the Radius to **5** to lessen the blur. The Radius setting controls the amount of blur.

Ⓒ Click **Close**.

11. **Save** your presentation.

Inserting a Screenshot

Video Lesson   labyrinthelab.com/videos

Sometimes you may want to include a picture of something, such as a program window or web page, on your computer screen in a presentation. PowerPoint's new Screenshot tool lets you insert a picture of any open window or program or drag on your screen to define an area to insert.

The Screenshot command is available on the Insert tab.

You can insert any open window as a picture.

Alternatively, you can drag on the screen to define an area to capture.

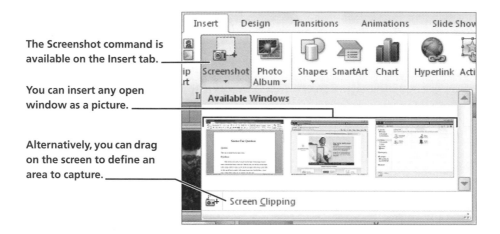

QUICK REFERENCE	INSERTING A SCREENSHOT
Task	**Procedure**
Insert a picture of an entire program window	■ Start the program or open the window you want to capture. ■ Return to PowerPoint and choose the slide on which to insert the picture. ■ Choose Insert→Images→Screenshot ▼menu→from the Ribbon. ■ Click the picture of the window you want to insert.
Insert a picture of a portion of the screen	■ Display the program or window you wish to insert. ■ Return to PowerPoint and choose the slide on which to insert the picture. ■ Choose Insert→Images→Screenshot ▼menu→Screen Clipping from the Ribbon. ■ Drag to define the area you wish to insert or tap Esc to leave the Screen Clipping tool.

3.3 Working with Shapes

Video Lesson labyrinthelab.com/videos

PowerPoint offers over 150 shapes that you can add to your slides. You can use these shapes to build your own custom flowcharts, mathematical equations, speech and thought bubbles, or other design. Shapes can even include text.

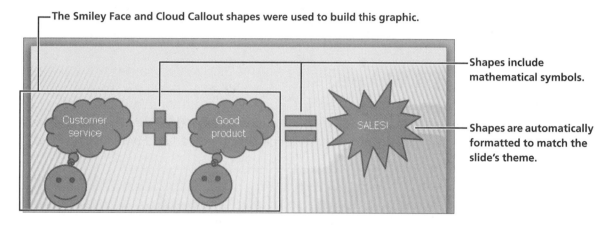

The Smiley Face and Cloud Callout shapes were used to build this graphic.

Shapes include mathematical symbols.

Shapes are automatically formatted to match the slide's theme.

Adding a Shape

When adding a shape to a slide, you can stretch it to make it wider/narrower or taller/shorter. All shapes are pre-formatted with a specific ratio of width to height, so stretching a shape can sometimes make it appear unbalanced. You can use the Shift key to maintain the original width-to-height ratio.

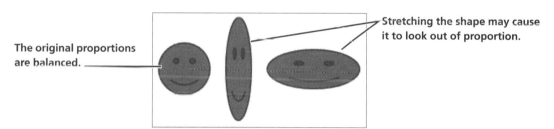

The original proportions are balanced.

Stretching the shape may cause it to look out of proportion.

Adding Text to a Shape

You can easily add text to a shape, but the text does not automatically resize itself to fit nicely. Text will, however, automatically wrap to the next line so there is no need to tap Enter as you type.

Text will automatically wrap to the next line but will not automatically get smaller to fit inside the shape.

You may need to adjust the text size to get it to fit.

Task	Procedure
Add a shape	▪ Choose Insert→Illustrations→Shapes ▼ from the Ribbon.
	▪ Select the shape you want and then drag on the slide to draw the shape.
	▪ Hold ⌈Shift⌉ as you drag the shape to maintain the original proportions.
Add text to a shape	▪ Add a shape to a slide.
	▪ With the shape selected and displaying a solid border, start typing. The text will automatically wrap to the next line when it reaches the edge of the shape, but it will not automatically resize itself to fit inside the shape.

Resizing a Shape

Shapes can be resized and rotated just like clip art. Additionally, some shapes include a yellow diamond that you can use to change the shape's properties. For example, you can change the Smiley Face shape to a frown or you can change the head and body of an arrow shape.

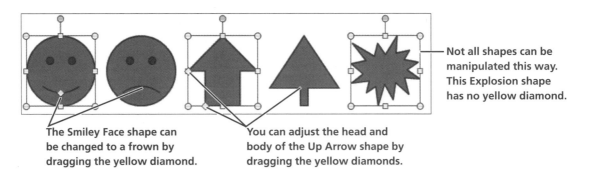

The Smiley Face shape can be changed to a frown by dragging the yellow diamond.

You can adjust the head and body of the Up Arrow shape by dragging the yellow diamonds.

Not all shapes can be manipulated this way. This Explosion shape has no yellow diamond.

Formatting Shapes and Shape Text

While shapes and the text they contain are automatically formatted to match the slide's theme, you may want a more exciting look such as a drop shadow or three-dimensional effect. Adding a Shape Style or WordArt Style can make your shape graphics really pop.

This is the original shape and text.

Here, a Shape Style and a WordArt Style have been applied to the shape and text.

Task	Procedure
Format a shape	■ Select the shape on the slide you wish to format.
	■ Choose a command from the Drawing Tools→Format→Shape Styles group on the Ribbon.
Format shape text	■ Select the shape on the slide containing the text you wish to format.
	■ Choose a command from the Drawing Tools→Format→WordArt Styles group on the Ribbon.

DEVELOP YOUR SKILLS 3.3.1

Add and Format a Shape with Text

In this exercise, you will add and format a shape with text.

Add a Shape with Text

1. Display the seventh slide, **Buster**.

2. Choose **Insert→Illustrations→Shapes ▼→Stars and Banners→5-Point Star** from the Ribbon.

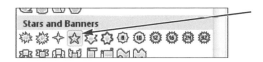

3. Hold Shift as you **drag** on the slide to create a star shape similar to the following figure.

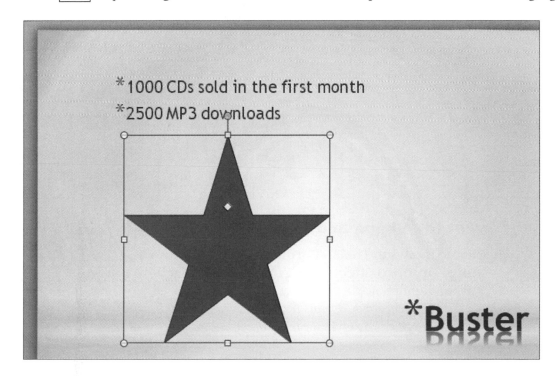

4. **Type** the following: `Top Seller!`
   Your star shape should resemble the following figure.

5. Click the **dashed border** of the shape so it turns solid.
   When the shape is selected, you can format its text.

6. Choose **Home→Font→Font Size ▼→44** from the Ribbon.
   The font size increases, but the text no longer fits nicely inside the shape. You will fix this in the next few steps.

Customize the Shape

7. Follow these steps to change the shape of the star and make the text fit nicely:

A Drag the **yellow diamond** up a little bit to change the shape of the star.

B Try to match your star shape to the figure. You may have to drag the yellow diamond up or down.

Format the Shape and Text

8. Choose **Drawing Tools→Format→Shape Styles→ More→Intense Effect – Red, Accent 6**. It is the bottom-right choice in the Shape Styles gallery.
   The shape changes color, appears three-dimensional, and displays a bottom reflection. However, the text remains the same.

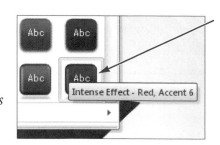

9. Choose **Drawing Tools→Format→WordArt Styles→More→Fill – White, Outline – Accent 1**. It is the fourth choice in the top row.

The text within the shape changes.

10. **Save**  your presentation.

3.4 Working with Slide Transitions

Video Lesson   labyrinthelab.com/videos

A slide transition is the animation between slides. Used properly, they can add zest and excitement to your presentation and provide a distinct breaking point between slides. PowerPoint 2010 includes many new transitions that are often used in video production, such as 3-D rotations and other animated effects.

The Vortex transition
occurring between two slides

Creating Transitions in Slide Sorter View

Most of the time, you will want to apply the same transition to the entire presentation. Using the Slide Sorter view is a quick and easy way to accomplish this task. You can apply transitions to a single slide, multiple slides, or all slides in a presentation. When you apply a transition, it animates the change from one slide to another, not individual elements of the slide.

Selecting Slides for Transitions

To easily select all slides in a presentation from Slide Sorter view, click to select the first slide in the presentation. If necessary, scroll to the bottom of the Slide Sorter window pane, press and hold the Shift key, click the last slide in the presentation, and then release the Shift key. All slides will be selected. After the slides are selected, choose Transitions→Transitions to This Slide from the Ribbon, and select a transition effect. The transition will be applied to all selected slides. You can also use this same method from the Normal view's Slides panel to select all slides in a presentation.

To apply a transition to a single slide, simply select a single slide in either Normal or Slide Sorter view, and then choose a slide transition from Transitions→Transitions to This Slide. The transition will be applied to the selected slide.

The Transitions Tab

The Transitions tab contains the Transitions to This Slide group, which you use to implement your slide transitions. The Transitions tab contains commands to apply transitions, sound, and other transition options to slides.

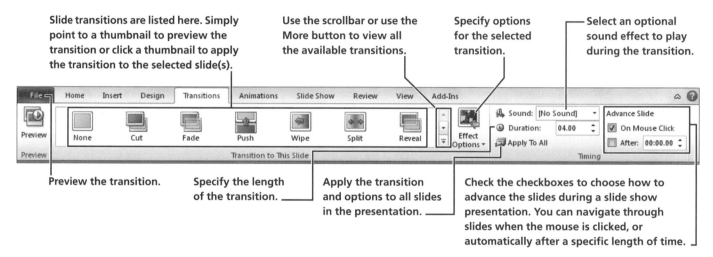

Slide transitions are listed here. Simply point to a thumbnail to preview the transition or click a thumbnail to apply the transition to the selected slide(s).

Use the scrollbar or use the More button to view all the available transitions.

Specify options for the selected transition.

Select an optional sound effect to play during the transition.

Preview the transition.

Specify the length of the transition.

Apply the transition and options to all slides in the presentation.

Check the checkboxes to choose how to advance the slides during a slide show presentation. You can navigate through slides when the mouse is clicked, or automatically after a specific length of time.

QUICK REFERENCE	ADDING TRANSITIONS TO A PRESENTATION
Task	**Procedure**
Add transitions to an entire presentation	■ From Slide Sorter view, press Ctrl+A to select all slides in a presentation. ■ Choose Transitions→Transition to This Slide and select the desired transition.
Set a transition for individual slides	■ Select the slide(s) to which you wish to apply a special transition. (Remember that transitions are seen when navigating to a slide when a slide loads.) ■ Choose Transitions→Transition to This Slide and select the desired transition.

Apply Transition Effects

In this exercise, you will apply the Vortex transition to all slides except the title slide.

Choose Transition Effects

1. Choose **View→Presentation Views→Slide Sorter** 🔲 from the Ribbon.

2. Choose the **Transitions** tab from the Ribbon.

3. Follow these steps to select multiple slides and choose a transition effect:

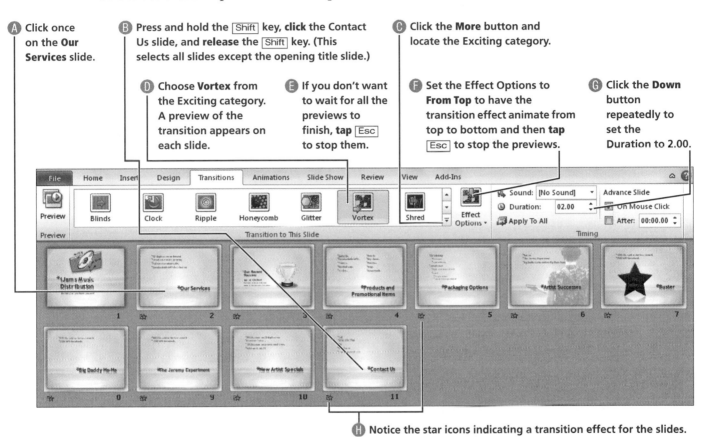

Ⓐ Click once on the **Our Services** slide.

Ⓑ Press and hold the [Shift] key, **click** the Contact Us slide, and **release** the [Shift] key. (This selects all slides except the opening title slide.)

Ⓒ Click the **More** button and locate the Exciting category.

Ⓓ Choose **Vortex** from the Exciting category. A preview of the transition appears on each slide.

Ⓔ If you don't want to wait for all the previews to finish, **tap** [Esc] to stop them.

Ⓕ Set the Effect Options to **From Top** to have the transition effect animate from top to bottom and then **tap** [Esc] to stop the previews.

Ⓖ Click the **Down** button repeatedly to set the Duration to 2.00.

Ⓗ Notice the star icons indicating a transition effect for the slides.

The title slide does not have the star icon because there is no transition applied to it.

Run the Presentation

4. Choose **Slide Show→Start Slide Show→From Beginning** 🖥 from the Ribbon.
   The title slide appears without a transition. The title slide would have opened with the Vortex transition if you had applied the transition to it.

5. Click the **mouse button** to advance to the next slide.
   The Vortex transition effect displays as the slides advance.

6. Continue to click the **mouse button** until you reach the end of the presentation and the Slide Sorter window reappears.

7. **Save** 💾 your presentation.

3.5 Using Slide Animation

Video Lesson   labyrinthelab.com/videos

Whereas transitions are applied to slides as a whole, animations are applied to individual objects *within* a slide. Animations begin only after any transition effect is completed. Some examples of animation include the following:

- A clip art image that moves across the slide to its final location
- A slide that starts out empty, and then has a heading and other elements that fade into view with a mouse click
- Bulleted paragraphs that fly in from the bottom of the slide one by one each time the presenter clicks with the mouse

Adding Animations

PowerPoint offers more than 40 animations you can add to objects on a slide by using a single command. For example, the Fade animation tells PowerPoint to gradually make objects on a slide fade into view after any transition effect is completed.

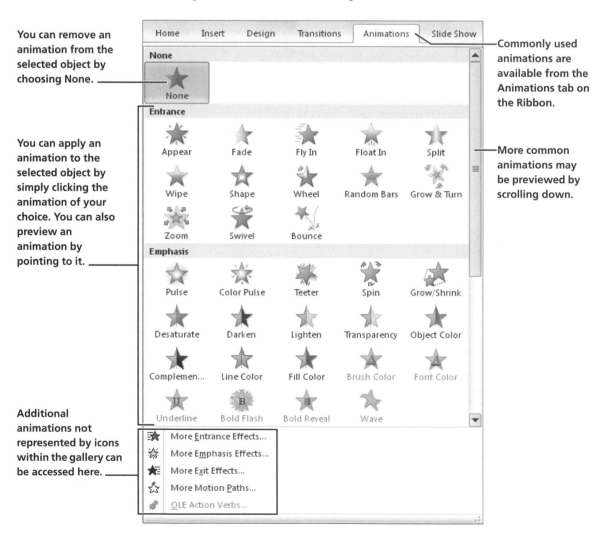

You can remove an animation from the selected object by choosing None.

Commonly used animations are available from the Animations tab on the Ribbon.

You can apply an animation to the selected object by simply clicking the animation of your choice. You can also preview an animation by pointing to it.

More common animations may be previewed by scrolling down.

Additional animations not represented by icons within the gallery can be accessed here.

Setting Animation Options

After applying an animation to an object, you will likely want to set the animation options to control exactly how the animation effect works. The available options differ based on whether the animation was applied to text or an image. The options also differ based on the animation itself. Additionally, you can set timing options to control the speed of the animation.

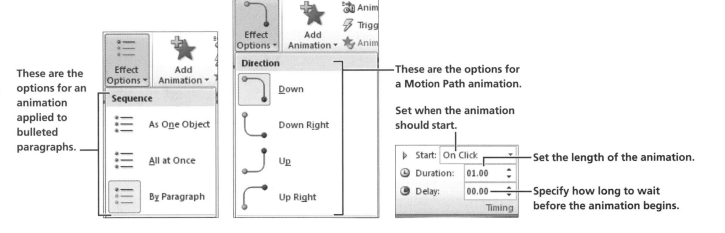

These are the options for an animation applied to bulleted paragraphs.

These are the options for a Motion Path animation.

Set when the animation should start.

Set the length of the animation.

Specify how long to wait before the animation begins.

QUICK REFERENCE	ADDING ANIMATION TO SLIDES
Task	**Procedure**
Apply a common animation to an object on a slide	■ Display the slide containing the object(s) to be animated. ■ Select the object (text object, picture, etc.) on the slide you wish to animate. ■ Choose Animations→Animation from the Ribbon. ■ Choose the desired animation from the menu.
Set animation options	■ Select the object containing the animation. ■ Choose Animation→Animation→Effect Options ▼ menu from the Ribbon. ■ Choose the desired option from the menu. ■ Set the options in the Animation→Timing group if desired.
Remove an animation	■ Select the object containing the animation. ■ Choose Animation→Animation→None from the Ribbon.

Apply Animation to Bulleted Paragraphs

In this exercise, you will apply an animation to text objects on a slide.

1. Choose **View→Presentation Views→Normal** from the Ribbon.

2. Display the **Our Services** slide.

3. Click once in the **bulleted text** so a dashed border appears around the text box.

4. Choose **Animations→Animation→More** $\boxed{\overline{}}$ **→Entrance→Float In**, as shown in the following figure.
   The animation previews, and you see each first-level paragraph animate across the slide.

5. Choose **Animations→Effect Option→Float Down** from the Ribbon to have the paragraphs animate from the top of the slide down.
   The numbers next to each bulleted paragraph indicate the order in which the animation is applied. By default, each paragraph will animate after a mouse click.

6. Choose **Slide Show→Start Slide Show→From Beginning** from the Ribbon to start the slide show.

7. **Click** anywhere with the mouse to advance to the second slide.
   The transition effect animates, but no bulleted paragraph appears yet.

8. **Click** anywhere with the mouse.
   The first bulleted paragraph animates into view.

9. Continue **clicking** until all four bulleted paragraphs are visible and the slide show advances to the third slide, Our Recent Success.

10. **Tap** $\boxed{\text{Esc}}$ to end the slide show and return to Normal view.

11. **Save** your presentation.

Using the Animation Pane

Video Lesson   labyrinthelab.com/videos

By using the Animation pane, you have many more choices for effects than you have in the animation menu you used previously. You can also individually set the animation for each element on a slide. When using the Animation pane, you can control the visual effects, timing, and sequencing of the animation process. For example, rather than having to click each time to display the next animated bulleted paragraph, you can set it so that the animation starts automatically after the slide transition and continues until all objects on the slide have been animated.

Budgeting Your Time

Using the Animation pane to customize each animation is a time consuming process. Be prepared to spend a significant amount of time selecting each animated object individually and then setting its options. The following figure describes the options on the Animation pane.

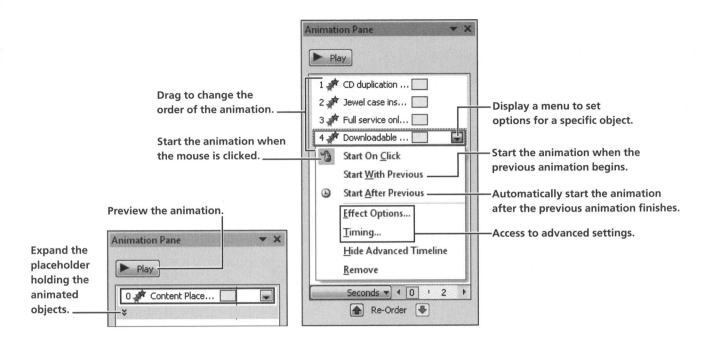

Drag to change the order of the animation.

Start the animation when the mouse is clicked.

Preview the animation.

Expand the placeholder holding the animated objects.

Display a menu to set options for a specific object.

Start the animation when the previous animation begins.

Automatically start the animation after the previous animation finishes.

Access to advanced settings.

Use the Animation Pane

In this exercise, you will use the Animation pane to configure the bulleted paragraphs to animate automatically after the slide transition completes.

1. Display the second slide, **Our Services**.

2. Click once in the **bulleted text** so a dashed border appears around the text box.

3. Choose **Animations→Advanced Animation→Animation Pane** from the Ribbon.
   The Animation pane displays on the right side of the screen.

4. Follow these steps to begin to configure the advanced animation settings:

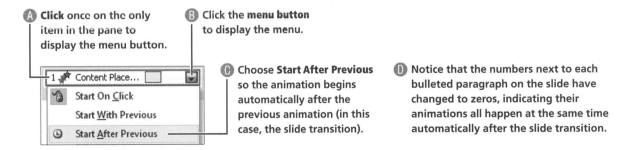

A **Click** once on the only item in the pane to display the menu button.

B Click the **menu button** to display the menu.

C Choose **Start After Previous** so the animation begins automatically after the previous animation (in this case, the slide transition).

D Notice that the numbers next to each bulleted paragraph on the slide have changed to zeros, indicating their animations all happen at the same time automatically after the slide transition.

5. Click the **Click to Expand Contents** bar to show each individual paragraph.

6. Follow these steps to customize the animation for the last paragraph:

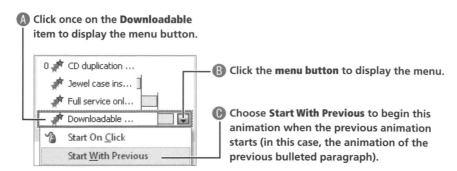

Ⓐ Click once on the **Downloadable** item to display the menu button.

Ⓑ Click the **menu button** to display the menu.

Ⓒ Choose **Start With Previous** to begin this animation when the previous animation starts (in this case, the animation of the previous bulleted paragraph).

7. Choose **Slide Show→Start Slide Show→From Beginning** from the Ribbon to start the slide show.

8. **Click** anywhere with the mouse to advance to the second slide.
   The bulleted paragraphs animate automatically after the slide transition ends. Each animation happens sequentially, except for the last bulleted paragraph, which animates with the previous item.

9. **Tap** Esc to end the slide show and return to Normal view.

10. **Save** your presentation.

3.6 Adding Sound Effects

Video Lesson   labyrinthelab.com/videos

PowerPoint 2010 provides audio clips and sound effects to accompany or accentuate your slide elements. For example, you may attach sound effects to slide transitions or animations. You can use the Transitions tab to add a sound to a slide transition or the Animation Pane to add a sound to an animation.

An example of a sound effect added to a slide transition

Adding a Sound Effect to an Animation

Sometimes you don't want a sound effect to play during a slide transition, but rather when an animation causes an object to move across the slide. The following illustration describes the steps used to apply sound effects to animations.

Select an object on the slide that has a custom animation applied.

In the Animation Pane, click the menu for the applied effect.

Choose Effect Options.

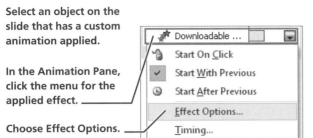

Select your sound effect from the dialog box and click the OK button.

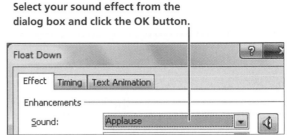

QUICK REFERENCE   **ADDING SOUND TO SLIDES**

Task	Procedure
Add sound to an animation	■ Display the slide with the animation to which you wish to add sound. Or add an animation to the slide object first. (You must create the animation before you can add sound to it.)
	■ Choose Animations→Advanced Animation→Animation Pane to display the Animation Pane.
	■ Click the menu button for the object to receive sound, and then choose Effect Options from the drop-down menu.
	■ In the Enhancements section of the dialog box, choose the sound you wish to apply, and then click OK.
Add sound to a transition	■ Select a slide from the Slides panel or Slide Sorter view.
	■ Choose Transitions→Timing→Sound menu and then select a sound effect. The sound will play as the selected slide loads.

DEVELOP YOUR SKILLS 3.6.1

Apply Sound Effects

In this exercise, you will apply two sounds to the presentation.

Apply a Sound Effect to an Animation

1. Choose the **Our Recent Success** slide, and then select the **clip art object**.

2. Choose **Animations→Animation→More→Entrance→Bounce** from the Ribbon to apply the Bounce animation to the trophy.

3. Click the **drop-down menu** for the clip art animation in the Animation Pane and choose **Effect Options**.

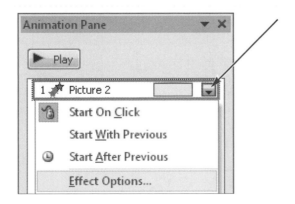

4. Click the **Sound** drop-down menu in the Effect tab and choose the **Applause** sound effect.

5. Click **OK**, and the animation and sound will be previewed.

Apply a Transition Sound Effect

6. Display the **Our Services** slide.

7. Follow these steps to add a transition sound effect:

Ⓐ Display the **Transitions** tab.

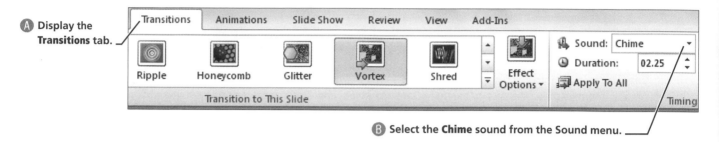

Ⓑ Select the **Chime** sound from the Sound menu.

PowerPoint applies the Chime sound to the transition effect for this slide.

8. Choose **Slide Show→Start Slide Show→From Beginning** 🖥 from the Ribbon.

9. **Navigate** through the presentation until you hear the applause and see the Bounce animation on the Our Recent Success slide.

You may not be able to hear the sound effect if your computer does not have speakers.

10. **Press** the ⌨Esc key to end the slide show early and return to Normal view.

11. **Close** the Animation Pane.

12. **Save** your presentation.

13. Choose **File→Close** to close the presentation.

3.7 Concepts Review

Concepts Review labyrinthelab.com/pp10

To check your knowledge of the key concepts introduced in this lesson, complete the Concepts Review quiz by going to the URL listed above. If your classroom is using Labyrinth eLab, you may complete the Concepts Review quiz from within your eLab course.

Reinforce Your Skills

Insert Clip Art

1. In this exercise, you will add clip art to the Tropical Getaways Animation presentation.

2. **Open** the rs-Tropical Getaways Animation presentation from your Lesson 03 folder.

3. Choose **View→Presentation Views→Normal** 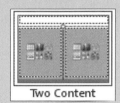 from the Ribbon.

4. Choose the **Travel Categories** slide (the second slide).

5. Choose **Home→Slides→Layout→Two Content**, as shown at right, to change the layout of the slide.

6. Click the **Clip Art** icon on the slide to display the Clip Art task pane.

7. Enter the keyword **vacation**.

8. Verify that Include **Office.com** content is checked and that Results Should Be is set to only **Illustrations**, and then click the **Go** button.

9. Choose a **clip art image** that appeals to you and click **OK**.
   If necessary, size and position your clip art image. Your slide may differ from the illustration.

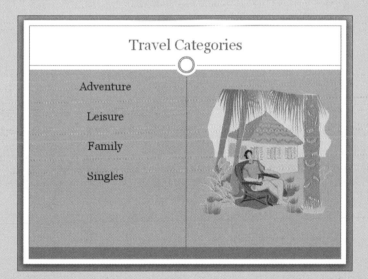

10. **Close** the Clip Art task pane.

11. **Save** your presentation and continue with the next exercise.

Format Clip Art

In this exercise, you will format clip art to add visual appeal to the presentation.

Before You Begin: The rs-Tropical Getaways Animation presentation from the previous exercise should be open.

1. Choose the **Travel Now and Save!** slide (the fifth slide).

2. Choose **Home→Slides→Layout→Two Content** to change the layout of the slide.

3. Click the **Clip Art** icon in the right column of the slide placeholder to display the Clip Art task pane.

4. Enter the keyword **tropics**.

5. Verify that **Include Office.com Content** is checked and that Results Should Be is set to only **Photographs**, and then click the **Go** button.

6. Choose a clip art **photograph** that appeals to you and click **OK**.
   If necessary, size and position your clip art photograph. Your slide may differ from the illustration.

7. Verify that the **photograph** is selected (you see its border with resize handles), and then choose **Format→Picture Styles→More** and select a style from the gallery.
   The illustration shows the Rotated White style applied. Your slide may differ.

8. **Close** the Clip Art task pane.

9. **Save** the changes to your presentation.

Apply Slide Transitions

In this exercise, you will apply slide transitions to your presentation.

Before You Begin: The rs-Tropical Getaways Animation presentation from the previous exercise should be open.

1. Choose **View→Presentation Views→Slide Sorter** from the Ribbon.

2. **Select** the first slide, and then ⎡Shift⎤+click the last slide.
   This selects all the slides in the presentation.

3. Choose **Transitions→Transition to This Slide→More** ⎡▾⎤, and then select a transition effect from the gallery.

4. If you are unhappy with your effect, choose **Transitions→Transition to This Slide→ More** and select a different transition.

5. **Save** your presentation.

Apply an Animation

In this exercise, you will animate bulleted paragraphs on a slide.

Before You Begin: The rs-Tropical Getaways Animation presentation from the previous exercise should be open.

1. Make sure you are in **Normal** view and choose the **Most Popular Destinations** slide (the third slide).

2. Select the **text object** on the left side of the slide.

3. Choose **Animations→Animation→More→Entrance→Grow & Turn** from the Ribbon.

4. Click in the **text** on the right side of the slide and apply the **Grow & Turn** animation.

5. **Save** your presentation.

Use the Animation Pane

In this exercise, you will animate clip art images with entry effects and sound.

Before You Begin: The rs-Tropical Getaways Animation presentation from the previous exercise should be open.

Animate the Vacation Image

1. Make sure you are in Normal view and choose the **Travel Categories** slide (the second slide).

2. Select the **clip art image**.

3. Choose **Animations→Animation→More→More Entrance Effects** from the Ribbon.

4. Scroll to the bottom of the **Change Entrance Effect** dialog box and choose the **Boomerang** effect as in the following figure, then click **OK**.

5. Choose **Animations→Advanced Animation→Animation Pane** from the Ribbon to display the Animation Pane.

6. Follow these steps to apply advanced options to the animation:

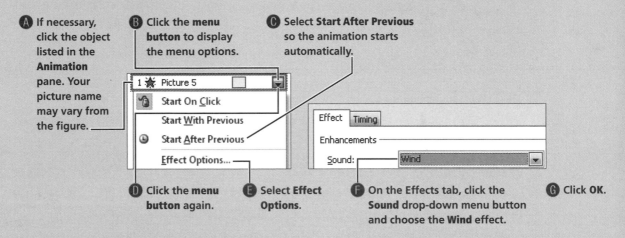

Animate the Tropics Image

7. Choose the **Travel Now and Save!** slide (the fifth slide).

8. Select the **photograph**.

9. Choose **Animations→Animation→More→More Entrance Effects** from the Ribbon.

10. Scroll down to the **Exciting** category, select the **Spiral In** effect, and click **OK**.

11. Use the **Animation Pane** to set the **Start** option to **Start After Previous**.

12. Apply a **sound effect** that you think works well with the photograph, such as the **Camera** effect.

13. **Close** the Animation Pane

14. Choose **Slide Show→Start Slide Show→From Beginning** from the Ribbon.

15. Work through the presentation, ensuring that the animation functions properly.

16. Feel free to add or modify the animation in your presentation.

17. **Save** the changes to the presentation and then **close** it.

Apply Your Skills

Remove the Background from a Picture

In this exercise, you will add a picture and remove the background.

1. **Open** the as-Classic Cars Animation presentation from the Lesson 03 folder.

2. Display the **Seminar Topics** slide.

3. Insert the **Classic Car** photo from the Lesson 03 folder.

4. Use the **Background Removal** tool to remove all but the yellow car from the picture and then **resize** the picture to fit on the slide. Your slide should resemble the following figure.

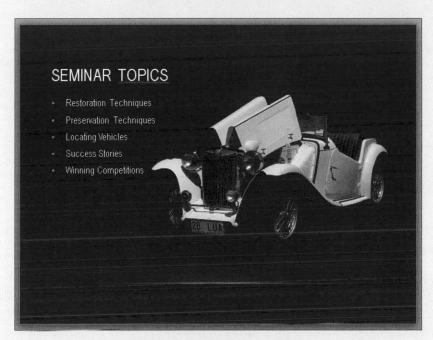

5. **Save** the presentation.

Insert and Format Clip Art

In this exercise, you will insert and format clip art.

Before you begin: *The as-Classic Cars Animation presentation from the previous exercise should be open.*

1. Select the **last slide**.

2. Use the **Clip Art** task pane to search for the phrase *classic car* and add an appropriate piece of clip art. Your slide may resemble this figure. Close the Clip Art task panel when you are finished.

3. Choose the **Format** tab and apply a **Picture Style** or **Picture Effect** to your image. The following figure shows the Half Reflection, Touching Picture Effect.

4. **Save** your presentation.

Add Slide Transitions to a Presentation

In this exercise, you will add slide transitions to the Classic Cars Animation presentation.

Before You Begin: The as-Classic Cars Animation presentation from the previous exercise should be open.

1. Display **Slide Sorter** view and select all slides in the presentation.

2. Display the **Transitions** tab and select a slide transition to be applied to every slide.

3. Choose **Slide Show→Start Slide Show→From Beginning** to test your transition. Change the transition effect if you are not happy with your current selection.

4. **Save** the presentation.

Add Animations to a Presentation

In this exercise, you will add animations to the Classic Cars Animation presentation.

Before You Begin: The as-Classic Cars Animation presentation from the previous exercise should be open.

1. Display **Normal** view and apply the **Zoom** animation to the bulleted paragraph on the **Seminar Topics** slide.

2. Use the following settings to apply an animation to the car picture on the Seminar Topics slide:
   - Use the **Random Bars** entrance effect.
   - Set the Effect Options to **Vertical**.
   - Set the Start time to **After Previous**.
   - Apply a **Chime** sound effect or some other effect that you prefer.

3. Use the following settings to apply custom animation to the clip art image on the closing slide:
   - Use the **Random Bars** entrance effect.
   - Set the animation to begin **after** the previous event has finished.
   - Set the Duration to **0.25**.
   - Apply a **Chime** sound effect or some other effect that you prefer.

4. **Run** the presentation when you have finished.

5. **Save** and **close** your presentation.

Critical Thinking & Work-Readiness Skills

In the course of working through the following Microsoft Office-based Critical Thinking exercises, you will also be utilizing various work-readiness skills, some of which are listed next to each exercise. Go to labyrinthelab.com/ workreadiness to learn more about the work-readiness skills.

3.1 Find and Use Clip Art

WORK-READINESS SKILLS APPLIED

- Serving clients/ customers
- Seeing things in the mind's eye
- Participating as a member of a team

Aurelia begins her project to, as Carthic says, "liven up" the presentation. "Customers—people—are very busy these days," he says. "I need to be able to attract and hold the attention of music lovers and the music press." Open ct-Clip Art (Lesson 03 folder). Find clip art with a musical meaning and insert it where you think it will work best. Try changing its size and rotating it. Save your final iteration of the file to your Lesson 03 folder as **ct-Clip Art Revised** and close it. If working in a group, discuss where else can you find clip art or other graphics you can use. If working alone, type your answer in a Word document named **ct-Questions** saved to your Lesson 03 folder.

3.2 Use Animation and Transitions

WORK-READINESS SKILLS APPLIED

- Thinking creatively
- Acquiring and evaluating information
- Participating as a member of a team

Carthic likes the clip art, but as he looks at the presentation again he says, "I think animation is very appropriate to our presentation. After all, music is often accompanied by motion of some kind—dancers or the musicians themselves. So, let's animate our logo or something along those lines—and have the slides themselves blend into each other. On the first slide and wherever there are bullet points, have the animations come in when I click rather than having them all together. OK?" Open ct-Clip Art Revised from your Lesson 03 folder and save it as **ct-Animation**. Make the changes Carthic suggests. Show the presentation to your instructor or to classmates for discussion.

3.3 Use Sound Clips

WORK-READINESS SKILLS APPLIED

- Serving clients/ customers
- Organizing and maintaining information
- Listening

Carthic practices with the new transitions Aurelia has put in and likes the dramatic effect. "There are three reasons I founded iJams," he says, practicing his speaking voice. He continues speaking, with each of the points sliding in as he clicks forward. "Great," he says, "but I have one request. Can you add a last slide with the title, 'Thanks for listening!' and put our URL (www.ijams.example.com), our 800 number, and my email carthic@ijams.example.com. Oh, and put drum sounds behind it." Open ct-Animation and insert a final slide, as described, and add a sound clip of drums. Save the presentation to your Lesson 03 folder as **ct-Sound**.

Inserting Charts

LEARNING OBJECTIVES

After studying this lesson, you will be able to:

- Insert charts to display numerical data
- Link to and use the data in an Excel spreadsheet to create a chart
- Format charts and change chart types
- Repair broken links to external documents
- Create SmartArt diagrams

A cornerstone of the Microsoft Office suite of programs is the seamless way programs join together, or integrate with each other. For example, in this lesson, you will learn how to place an Excel workbook into a PowerPoint presentation to harness the strength of Excel features in PowerPoint. You will also take advantage of the Microsoft Graph charting program to create dynamic and precise charts in your presentation. Last, you will use SmartArt to add a beautifully arranged organization chart that is clear, concise, and stylish.

Case Study

Working as a team, Carthic and Aurelia continue to develop PowerPoint presentations for iJams. With the combination of Aurelia's skill in fine-tuning the presentation and Carthic's dynamic delivery style, with each presentation they win more customers to iJams. Finally, Carthic decides it is time to expand iJams by opening a recording studio that local musicians can rent to record their original music. He schedules a meeting with the loan committee at Twilight Hollow Bank. Carthic is concerned that he will have to re-create his best Excel workbook of financial projections until Aurelia reminds him that they can simply link the Excel file to the PowerPoint presentation.

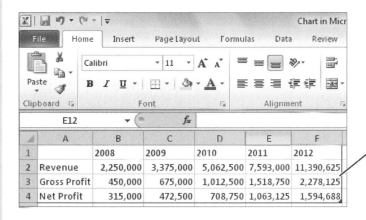

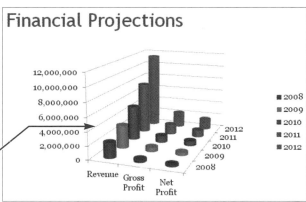

4.1 Inserting Charts

Video Lesson   labyrinthelab.com/videos

PowerPoint is an intensely visual application. Although it is often the case that you will be creating presentations that represent concepts or goals, there are also times when you will need to present financial statistics or numerical data. PowerPoint allows you to create charts based on numerical data in a spreadsheet. If Microsoft Excel is installed, PowerPoint and Excel will work together to provide you with advanced options to design the chart layout and edit chart data. Without Excel installed, PowerPoint will use Microsoft Graph to create a new chart. Excel offers the more intuitive Ribbon interface, provides more formatting options, and creates more visually appealing charts than Microsoft Graph. Therefore, it is recommended that you use Excel to create charts for your PowerPoint presentations. In fact, if Excel is installed, PowerPoint launches it automatically whenever you insert a new chart.

This lesson assumes that both PowerPoint and Excel were part of your Office Suite installation.

Creating Embedded Charts

PowerPoint supplies you with four layouts (Title and Content, Two Content, Comparison, and Content with Caption) that make inserting new charts simple. Each of these common layouts includes an Insert Chart icon that you can click to insert a new chart. What if your slide doesn't use one of these layouts? You can always insert a chart manually from the Ribbon, no matter what layout your slide uses.

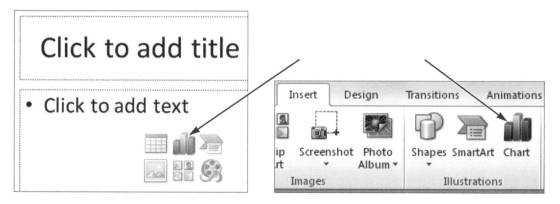

You can insert a chart via the Insert Chart slide icon or from the Ribbon.

Microsoft Graph

If Excel is not installed, PowerPoint launches a Microsoft Graph datasheet when you insert a new chart. (Microsoft Graph is a small program installed with many Office applications.) Charts created in Microsoft Graph lack the Chart Tools contextual Ribbon tabs and commands that are available with an Excel-generated chart for advanced formatting and easy editing (these tabs are discussed later in this lesson). A Microsoft Graph chart can be converted to Office 2010 format, which results in the contextual Ribbon tabs being made available and chart data editing handled by Excel. However, without Excel installed, a converted chart is not editable. The rest of this lesson assumes that you have Excel installed.

To convert a Microsoft Graph chart to Office 2010 format, double-click the chart on the slide and choose Convert. However, remember that Excel must be installed to edit numeric data in a converted chart.

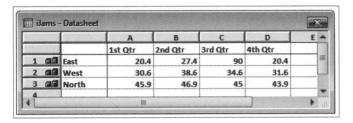

Microsoft Graph datasheet

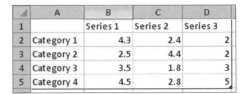

Excel spreadsheet

When you insert a new chart, PowerPoint starts you out with generic data labels and numbers that you replace with your own.

Choosing a Chart Type

Certain types of charts are best suited to display specific types of data. Some of the most commonly used chart types are described in the following table.

Chart Type	Icon	Best Used to...
Column	Column	Show one-time (nonadjacent) results, such as those of a survey. A column chart uses vertical bars
Bar	Bar	Show the same type of results as a column chart, but with horizontal bars
Line	Line	Show continual change over time, such as profit/loss over several months
Pie	Pie	Compare a portion or portions to a whole, such as hours spent on various tasks in a single day

Editing Chart Data

When you create a new chart, PowerPoint automatically launches the Excel spreadsheet application if it is installed on your computer. This allows you to take advantage of Excel's powerful tools for working with numeric data. Don't be confused when you insert a new chart only to see data already entered in the Excel spreadsheet window—this is sample data that PowerPoint inserts to get you started. Simply replace this data with your own headings and numbers.

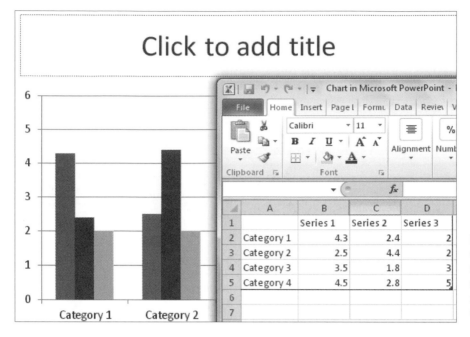

Excel opens and displays a datasheet with sample data when you first insert a new chart. You simply replace the sample data with the real data.

Formatting Charts

After a chart has been inserted from Excel, simply click the chart to select it. PowerPoint's Chart Tools are displayed in the Ribbon as the Design, Layout, and Format contextual tabs. You can use these tabs to create, modify, and format your chart without leaving the PowerPoint window. The following illustration shows the PowerPoint window as an Excel-generated chart being inserted.

The Design, Layout, and Format contextual tabs display whenever a chart is selected.

DEVELOP YOUR SKILLS 4.1.1

Insert a Chart

In this exercise, you will create a chart inside your PowerPoint presentation and revise the default datasheet with your own custom data.

> **NOTE** The instructions for this and other charting exercises assume that Excel 2010 is installed on your computer.

Insert the Slide and Add Text

1. **Open** the iJams presentation from the Lesson 04 folder on your file storage location.

2. Display **slide 3**, Our Expansion Plan, via the Slides pane.
   In the next few steps, you will add a new slide after Our Expansion Plan.

3. Choose **Home→Slides→New Slide** 📇 from the Ribbon.

4. Choose **Home→Slides→** 📇 Layout ▾ **→Two Content** from the Ribbon.
   PowerPoint will apply the new layout, which includes a placeholder box on the left that you will use for your text, and a placeholder box on the right that you will use for your chart.

5. Type **Year-To-Date Results** as the title.

6. Click in the **placeholder** box on the left side and add the following **bulleted text items**, **pressing** ⎗Enter⎘ after each one except the last:

   - **25% growth rate** ⎗Enter⎘
   - **Positive cash flow** ⎗Enter⎘
   - **Margins increasing**

Set Up the Chart

7. Click the **Insert Chart** 📊 icon in the middle of the placeholder box on the right side.
   The Insert Chart dialog box appears. Knowing the type of data you are charting will make it easier to select the appropriate type of chart. You are charting one-time results, so a column or bar graph is most appropriate.

8. Follow these steps to insert a chart from the Insert Chart dialog box:

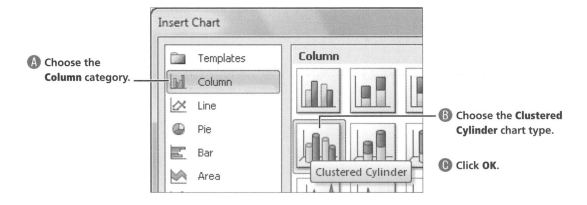

Ⓐ Choose the **Column** category.

Ⓑ Choose the **Clustered Cylinder** chart type.

Ⓒ Click **OK**.

Excel opens with sample data. You will replace the sample data with your own headings and numbers.

9. Follow these steps to set up the chart datasheet:

(A) Click the cell with the text Category 1 and type **Q1**, and then **tap** Enter. The text *Q1* will replace the text *Category 1*.

(B) **Enter** the remaining data shown here, except for the bottom row labeled Category 4. **Click** a cell, **type** the cell data, and then **click** another cell.

⊿	A	B	C	D	E	F	G
1		Net Profits	Gross Profi	Revenue			
2	Q1	60000	78000	350000			
3	Q2	65000	85000	400000			
4	Q3	72000	90000	430000			
5	Category 4	4.5	2.8	5			

(C) Point to the **left** of the bottom row until your mouse pointer turns into an arrow, and then **click** once to select the row and **tap** Delete. (You don't need this extra row of data.)

(D) In the Excel window, choose **File→Exit** to close the datasheet and return to the PowerPoint slide.

Your slide should now resemble the following illustration. Notice how tightly squeezed the chart appears. In the next topic, you will learn how to modify a chart to aid readability and make it visually attractive.

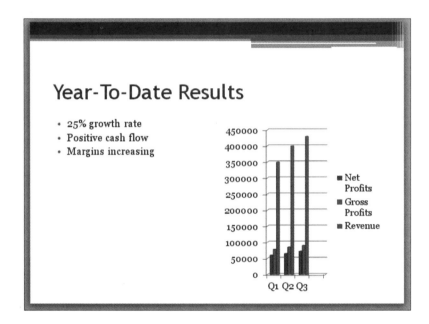

10. **Save**  your presentation and continue with the next topic.

Modifying Charts

Video Lesson labyrinthelab.com/videos

After you insert a chart, you can make all sorts of changes to it as necessary. For example, you can edit the chart data, change the color scheme, and even change to a different chart type. As you would expect, the three Chart Tools contextual tabs on the Ribbon give access to these modification commands.

Chart Tools		
Design	Layout	Format

If you don't see the Chart Tools contextual tabs, make sure that the chart is selected (displays sizing handles).

118 Lesson 4: Inserting Charts

Changing the Chart Size and Layout

You can size the chart by dragging the sizing handles, and you can position the chart by dragging it to a different location. These handles work just as they do on clip art and other figures on slides. You can also choose a different layout for the chart from the Design tab under Chart Tools.

Editing Chart Data

When you edit data in a chart on a PowerPoint slide, PowerPoint automatically launches the Excel spreadsheet program. When you have finished editing chart data, close Excel or click anywhere in the PowerPoint window to hide Excel and restore the PowerPoint window.

Changing the Chart Type and Color Scheme

Sometimes you may want to change the chart type to better display the data. For example, you might want to switch from a normal bar chart to a 3-D style bar chart. Or, you may want to use a stacked bar chart style if space is limited on the slide. Additionally, you can change the chart's layout and reposition the chart's text components around the chart graphic.

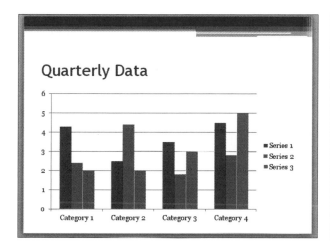
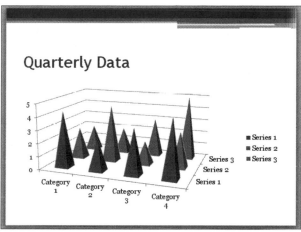

The same chart data first displayed as a Clustered Column, then as a 3-D Pyramid

QUICK REFERENCE	CHARTING IN POWERPOINT
Task	**Procedure**
Insert a chart	■ Click the Insert Chart [icon] icon on the slide, or choose Insert→Illustrations→Chart from the Ribbon.
Change the size of a chart	■ Point to a sizing handle around the chart's border until your mouse pointer turns into a double-headed arrow, and then click and drag the border.
Change the chart type	■ Select the chart. ■ Choose Chart Tools→Design→Type→Change Chart Type [icon] from the Ribbon.
Modify chart data	■ Select the chart. ■ Choose Chart Tools→Design→Data→Edit Data [icon] from the Ribbon.
Change the chart layout	■ Select the chart. ■ Choose a layout from the Chart Tools→Design→Chart Layouts command group from the Ribbon.

Modify a Chart

In this exercise, you will modify the chart slide by adjusting its size and editing the chart data.

1. Follow these steps to resize the chart:

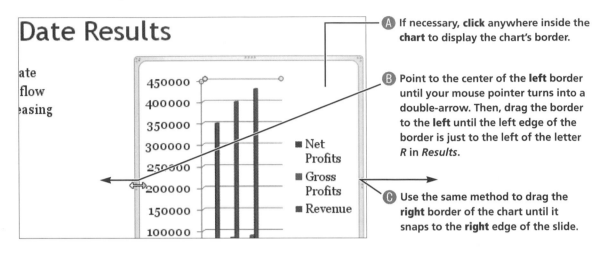

(A) If necessary, **click** anywhere inside the **chart** to display the chart's border.

(B) Point to the center of the **left** border until your mouse pointer turns into a double-arrow. Then, drag the border to the **left** until the left edge of the border is just to the left of the letter *R* in *Results*.

(C) Use the same method to drag the **right** border of the chart until it snaps to the **right** edge of the slide.

You have resized the chart but have maintained some breathing room (white space) between the left border of the chart and the bulleted text. You have also maintained some white space between the right edge of the chart and the slide's right edge.

2. Make sure that the chart is still selected and that the Chart Tools contextual tabs are visible.

3. Choose **Chart Tools→Design→Data→Edit Data** from the Ribbon to display the datasheet in Excel.
This type of chart is an embedded object. You can always edit the data in an embedded chart by selecting this command.

4. Follow these steps to edit the chart in Excel:

(A) Click in the 60000 cell, and then type **160000** and tap Enter .

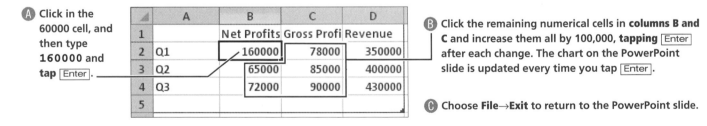

(B) Click the remaining numerical cells in **columns B and C** and increase them all by 100,000, **tapping** Enter after each change. The chart on the PowerPoint slide is updated every time you tap Enter .

(C) Choose **File→Exit** to return to the PowerPoint slide.

Now let's change the chart type to a more visually interesting style.

5. Follow these steps to change the chart type:

Ⓐ Make sure that the **Design** contextual tab is displayed under Chart Tools. (Select the chart again if necessary to make the Chart Tools contextual tabs visible.) ⎯

Ⓑ Choose the **Change Chart Type** command. ⎯

Ⓒ Double-click the **3-D Cylinder** in the Column chart type group. ⎯

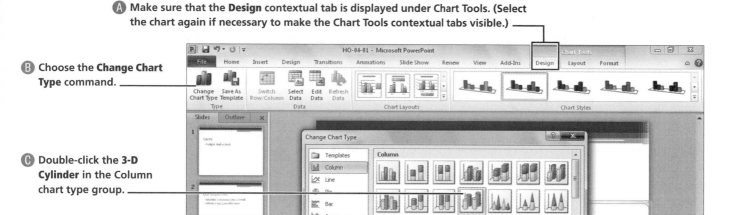

The chart type changes, but it is difficult to read. The bars in the graph are too congested, and the text is difficult to read.

6. Choose **Chart Tools→Design→Chart Layouts→Layout 3** as shown in the following illustration.

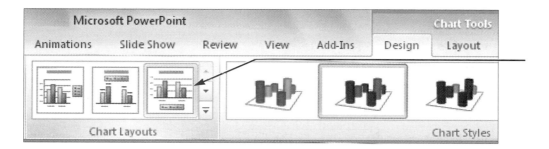

PowerPoint rearranges the slide layout to add a title and place the legend below the chart. The slide itself has a title, so we will delete the additional title inside the chart.

7. Click once on the **Chart Title** so it displays handles, and then **tap** the ⌊Delete⌋ key.

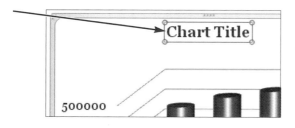

The chart title disappears. Your slide should resemble the following illustration.

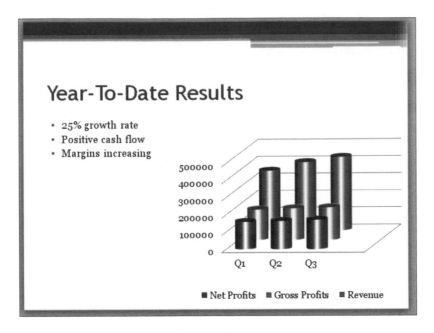

8. **Save** 🖫 your presentation and continue with the next topic.

4.2 Working with External Excel Documents

Video Lesson   labyrinthelab.com/videos

Office 2010 provides a variety of tools and techniques to let you exchange data between applications. Object Linking and Embedding (OLE) allows you to create links between source documents and destination documents. For example, you may want a chart in an existing Excel document to appear in a PowerPoint presentation. This makes it possible for another individual or department to maintain the Excel spreadsheet and its numerical data while you simply link to it and display an attractive chart based on its contents.

Benefits of Linking

Creating a chart in Excel and linking the chart object to PowerPoint gives you the opportunity to maintain modularity over presentation components. The Excel data remains in the Excel spreadsheet, which can be maintained by the financial wizards, while the PowerPoint presentation remains totally under your control as a separate document. Any changes made to the Excel document can be reflected in the chart displayed on the PowerPoint slide. Don't be worried if, during your actual presentation, the Excel spreadsheet is not available. The chart will still display beautifully. The Excel spreadsheet needs to be available only if you want to edit the chart data.

Changes to the Excel spreadsheet data here...

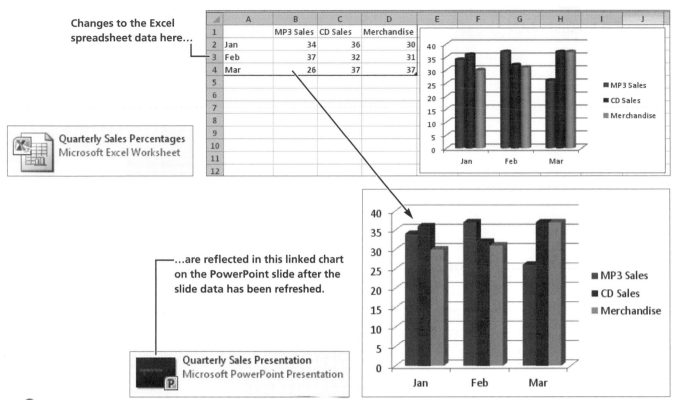

Quarterly Sales Percentages
Microsoft Excel Worksheet

...are reflected in this linked chart on the PowerPoint slide after the slide data has been refreshed.

Quarterly Sales Presentation
Microsoft PowerPoint Presentation

Changes to a linked Excel document *do not* result in automatic updating of the PowerPoint chart; you must manually refresh the PowerPoint chart's data to see the updated content.

Only Data Is Linked

A linked chart on a PowerPoint slide is linked to the *data* in the Excel spreadsheet, not to the chart within Excel. The chart on the Excel spreadsheet simply establishes the initial link to its data. So, deleting or changing the format of the Excel chart has no effect on the chart on the PowerPoint slide. In the preceding illustration, notice that the formatting on the Excel chart is quite different from that on the PowerPoint slide. This independence is very useful because it allows PowerPoint to format the chart so it is consistent with the presentation theme's colors and fonts.

Linking Excel Charts

Your first step in linking to an Excel spreadsheet is to create (or have someone create) the Excel spreadsheet that contains numerical data and an Excel chart. You simply copy and paste the chart (not the spreadsheet cells containing numerical data) from the Excel spreadsheet into your slide. The chart on the PowerPoint slide will be linked to the Excel spreadsheet's numerical data by default.

Task	Procedure
Link a chart	■ Select the chart on the Excel spreadsheet and choose Home→Clipboard→Copy from the Ribbon.
	■ Select the desired slide in PowerPoint and choose Home→Clipboard→Paste from the Ribbon.
Edit linked data	■ Select the chart on the slide.
	■ Choose Chart Tools→Design→Data→Edit Data from the Ribbon.
	■ If available, the linked document will open. Edit the data in the Excel spreadsheet, not on the Excel chart, and save your changes.
Refresh chart data linked to an external file	■ Select the chart on the PowerPoint slide.
	■ Choose Chart Tools→Design→Data→Refresh Data from the Ribbon.
Repair a broken link	■ Select the chart.
	■ Choose File→Info and then click the Edit Links to Files link at the bottom of the right column.
	■ Click the Change Source button.
	■ Navigate to the source file, select it, and click Open.
	■ Click the Close button.

DEVELOP YOUR SKILLS 4.2.1

Link to an Excel Chart

In this exercise, you will link to an existing Excel chart. You will then edit the Excel data to update the chart in PowerPoint.

Copy the Chart Object from Excel

1. Choose **Start→All Programs→Microsoft Office→Microsoft Office Excel 2010**.
   The Excel program loads and the Excel window appears.

2. Choose **File→Open**.

3. Navigate to the Lesson 04 folder and **open** the iJams Financial Projections spreadsheet.

4. Click anywhere on the **Excel** chart to select it.
   A border appears around the chart to indicate that it has been selected.

5. Choose **Home→Clipboard→Copy** 📋 from the Ribbon.

6. Choose **File→Exit**.
   Excel closes, and you are returned to the PowerPoint window.

Link the Chart to PowerPoint

7. Choose the **Year-To-Date Results** slide.

8. Choose **Home→Slides→New Slide** 🗔 from the Ribbon.

9. Choose **Home→Slides→ 🔲 Layout ▾ →Title Only**.
   The new slide's layout is converted to the Title Only layout.

10. Click the **title box** of the new slide and type `Financial Projections`, and then **click** below the title in a blank area of the slide.
The title box becomes deselected.

11. Choose **Home→Clipboard→Paste** 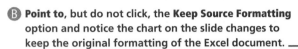 from the Ribbon.
PowerPoint pastes the chart into the slide.

12. Follow these steps to explore the paste options on the slide:

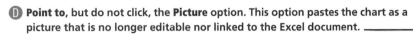

Ⓐ Click the **Paste Options** button in the bottom-right corner of the chart.

Ⓑ **Point to,** but do not click, the **Keep Source Formatting** option and notice the chart on the slide changes to keep the original formatting of the Excel document.

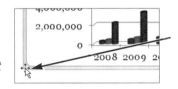

Ⓒ **Point to,** but do not click, the **Use Destination Theme** option and notice the chart inherits the formatting of the current PowerPoint theme. This is the default setting.

Ⓓ **Point to,** but do not click, the **Picture** option. This option pastes the chart as a picture that is no longer editable nor linked to the Excel document.

Ⓔ Click the **Paste Options** button again to close the options menu without changing the default selection (Use Destination Theme).

Resize the Chart

Now you will resize the chart so it fits your slide well.

13. Point to the chart's **border** until your mouse pointer becomes a four-headed arrow. Then **drag** the chart to the lower-left corner of the slide.
Note that the chart snaps into position as the lower-left corner of the chart approaches the lower-left corner of the slide.

14. Follow these steps to resize the chart:

Ⓐ Point to the **middle-right** resize handle on the chart border until your mouse pointer becomes a double white arrow, and then **drag** the border to the right edge of the slide.

Ⓑ Using this same method, drag the **top** of the chart border until it is just below the slide title.

Your slide should now appear similar to the following illustration. The chart's text is too small to read comfortably. You will fix that in the next steps.

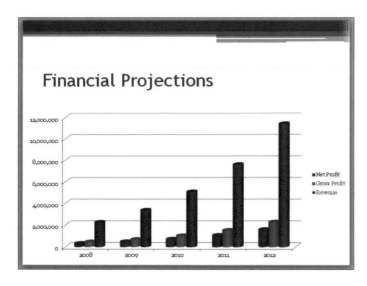

Format the Chart

15. Make sure the chart is selected and its border is displayed, and then choose **Home→Font→Font Size ▾ menu→20**.
    All text on the chart is enlarged to size 20.

16. Click once on the **legend** to the right of the chart to select the text block.
    We will change the color of each legend entry to match the color scheme of the chart's bars.

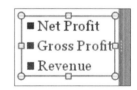

17. With the legend block selected, **click** once on the first item in the legend, **Net Profit**.

18. Choose **Home→Font→Font Color ▾ menu** and select the seventh color, **Purple Accent 3**, along the top row. This matches the purple in the document theme, which is used for the Net Profit bullet and chart bar.
    If your colors are different from those in the figure, choose the color that matches the square bullet to the left of Net Profit.

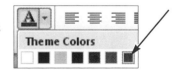

19. Click once on the second item in the legend, **Gross Profit**.

20. Choose **Home→Font→Font Color ▾ menu** and select the sixth color, **Teal Accent 2**, along the top row. This matches the green in the document theme, which is used for the Gross Profit bullet and chart bar.

21. Select the last item in the legend, **Revenue**, and change its color to the shade of indigo used in the document theme.

The chart text is now larger and easier to read, and the chart legend is color-coded to match the chart's bars. Your slide should resemble the following illustration.

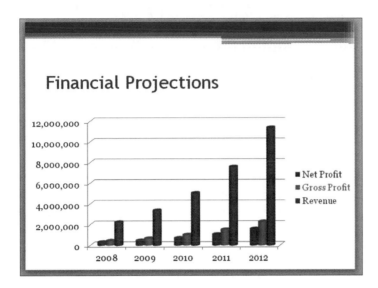

22. **Save** 💾 your presentation and continue with the next topic.

Effects of Linking

| **Video Lesson** | labyrinthelab.com/videos |

When you paste a linked chart, any changes made to the Excel spreadsheet are reflected in the chart on the PowerPoint slide after the chart data is refreshed in PowerPoint. If you choose to paste unlinked, changes to the Excel spreadsheet will have no effect on the chart in the Power-Point slide. If you attempt to edit the chart data from within PowerPoint, Excel will open and present the linked spreadsheet ready for editing. If the linked spreadsheet cannot be found, you will not be able to edit the chart data until the link is repaired.

DEVELOP YOUR SKILLS 4.2.2
Edit Data in a Linked Spreadsheet

In this exercise, you will edit the data in a linked Excel spreadsheet.

1. Select the **Financial Projections** slide if necessary, click the chart to select it, and then choose **Chart Tools→Design→Data→Edit Data** from the Ribbon.
   Excel launches and opens the data source for the chart.

2. If necessary, maximize the **Excel** window so the data and Ribbon are visible.

3. Follow these steps to edit the chart data:

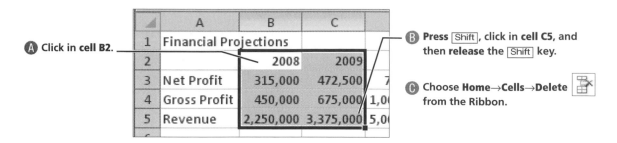

(A) Click in **cell B2**.

(B) Press ⌈Shift⌉, click in **cell C5**, and then **release** the ⌈Shift⌉ key.

(C) Choose **Home→Cells→Delete** from the Ribbon.

Excel deletes the data in your selection.

4. **Save** 💾 the spreadsheet.

5. Choose **File→Exit**.
Excel closes, and you are returned to the PowerPoint window.

6. **Save** 💾 your presentation.

7. Choose **File→Close** to close your presentation while leaving PowerPoint open.

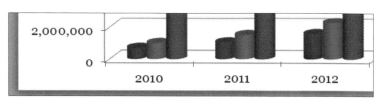

The final slide

In the next exercise, you will edit linked data while your presentation is not open.

Editing the Source (Linked) Document

Video Lesson   labyrinthelab.com/videos

If you make a change to the source document when PowerPoint is closed, you must manually refresh the data when you open your presentation. Refreshing data is only possible if you have healthy links. You'll do this in the next activity.

DEVELOP YOUR SKILLS 4.2.3
Edit and Refresh the Data Source

In this exercise, you will edit and refresh the data source.

Before You Begin: PowerPoint should be open but your iJams presentation is closed.

Edit the Data Source

1. Choose **Start→All Programs→Microsoft Office→Microsoft Office Excel 2010**.
The Excel window appears.

2. Choose **File→Open**. Then, navigate to the Lesson 04 folder and **open** the file iJams Financial Projections.

3. Click in **cell A5** and type **Big Money**.
Excel replaces the word Revenue *with* Big Money.

4. **Save** 💾 the worksheet and **exit** Excel.

Refresh the Data Source

5. In **PowerPoint**, click the **File** tab, and then choose **iJams** from the Recent Presentations list in the right panel.
   This list is a handy way to reopen your most recent work in any Office application.

6. Display the last slide, **Financial Projections**.
   Notice that the chart legend to the right of the chart still shows the word Revenue. *It must be refreshed to reflect the changes in the data source.*

7. Select the chart so the **Chart Tools** contextual tabs appear.

8. Choose **Chart Tools→Design→Data→Refresh Data**  from the Ribbon.
   PowerPoint refreshes the chart legend and now shows the phrase Big Money.

9. **Save** 💾 your presentation and continue to the next topic.

Maintaining Healthy Links

Video Lesson labyrinthelab.com/videos

Linked objects can reflect changes in the source document only if the link is maintained. Moving files to other locations on your file system or renaming files can lead to broken links, and your linked objects (like charts) will no longer reflect changes made to the source document.

 If you try to edit chart data and the Excel spreadsheet fails to open, chances are you have a broken link. You'll need to repair it before you can edit data from within PowerPoint.

Example

For example, if you copied a chart from an Excel spreadsheet named Chart Data that was stored in a folder named My Excel Documents, PowerPoint would be looking for a file with that name in that location. If you moved the Excel file (or the containing folder) to another folder or changed its name, PowerPoint would no longer be able to find it; therefore, any changes made to the spreadsheet would have no effect on the chart in PowerPoint. And if you tried to edit the data from within PowerPoint, PowerPoint would not be able to find the Excel spreadsheet and thus would not be able to edit the data.

The following figure illustrates the prompt that PowerPoint displays if you break a link to an external file—for example, if you move or rename the data source file, and then try to edit a chart from PowerPoint.

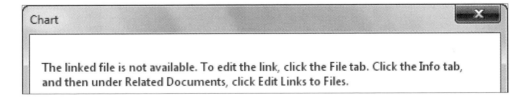

Break and Repair a Link

In this exercise, you will break a link by renaming the linked data file, and then you will repair the link from within PowerPoint.

Before You Begin: The iJams presentation is open in PowerPoint.

1. **Minimize** ▬ the PowerPoint window to the taskbar.

2. Follow the instructions for your version of Windows to open a window for your file storage location:

   ■ **Win XP**: Use **Start→My Computer**, and then open your file storage location.

   ■ **Win Vista/7**: Use **Start→Computer**, and then open your file storage location.

3. **Open** the folder where you store your exercise files, and then **open** the Lesson 04 folder.

 In the next step, you will rename a file. Most windows systems hide the end of filenames (called the extension). If filename extensions are visible in the folder window, you must take care not to change them.

4. Follow these steps to rename the Excel worksheet file:

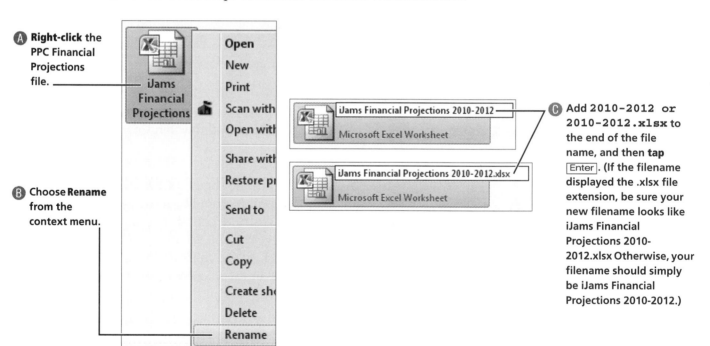

A **Right-click** the PPC Financial Projections file.

B Choose **Rename** from the context menu.

C Add **2010-2012** or **2010-2012.xlsx** to the end of the file name, and then **tap** Enter. (If the filename displayed the .xlsx file extension, be sure your new filename looks like iJams Financial Projections 2010-2012.xlsx Otherwise, your filename should simply be iJams Financial Projections 2010-2012.)

By renaming the source document, you have broken its link to PowerPoint.

5. Click the **PowerPoint** button on the Windows taskbar to restore PowerPoint to the screen.

6. Click the **chart** to select it, if necessary.

7. Choose **Chart Tools→Design→Data→Edit Data** 📊 from the Ribbon.
   You receive an error. PowerPoint is looking for a source document named iJams Financial Projections, but you changed the name of the file.

8. Click the **OK** button in the error box.

Fix the Broken Link

Now that you've broken the link by renaming the file, you will see how easy it is to repair the link.

9. Choose **File→Info** and then click the **Edit Links to Files** command at the bottom-right of the right column, as shown in the following illustration.

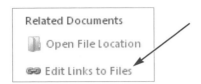

   The Links dialog box appears, listing all links to external files from the presentation. In this case, there is just one linked item, the Excel spreadsheet.

10. Click the **Change Source** button.

11. In the **Change Source** dialog box, navigate to the Lesson 04 folder, select the iJams Financial Projections 2010-2012 file, and click the **Open** button.
    PowerPoint updates the link. There may not be enough space in the dialog box to make the new name visible.

12. **Click** [Close] to close the Links dialog box.
    You have reestablished the link between the PowerPoint chart and the Excel source document.

Test the Repaired Link

13. Click **File** to close Backstage View and then click the **chart** to select it, if necessary.
    The chart must be selected in order to display the Chart Tools contextual tabs.

14. Choose **Chart Tools→Design→Data→Edit Data** ⊞ from the Ribbon.
    The source document opens, ready to edit.

15. Click in **cell A5**. Then type **Revenue** and tap [Enter].
    Excel replaces Big Money with the new word.

16. **Save** 💾 the Excel document and then **exit** Excel.

17. **Save** 💾 your presentation and continue with the next topic.

4.3 Creating SmartArt Diagrams

Video Lesson   labyrinthelab.com/videos

SmartArt graphics are diagrams that automatically resize to accommodate the text within and allow the average user to enhance slides with visually appealing figures without having to learn advanced graphics software. With SmartArt, you simply select the type of diagram you'd like to create and type your text. The SmartArt diagram automatically sizes and flows your text. It also inherits colors and 3-D effects from your document theme. The resulting diagrams can help crystallize concepts in your presentation so that the audience will clearly understand your ideas. Using SmartArt, you can add graphics to your presentations such as:

- Organization charts
- Flowcharts
- Colorful lists
- And many other sophisticated graphics

Inserting and Formatting SmartArt Graphics

Most slide layouts include an Insert SmartArt Graphic icon. Alternatively, SmartArt can be inserted at any time via the Ribbon. When you click the Insert SmartArt Graphic icon, the Choose a SmartArt Graphic dialog box appears. You can choose a diagram type from the gallery and then construct the diagram directly on the slide. PowerPoint displays examples and descriptions of the various SmartArt graphics as you select them in the gallery.

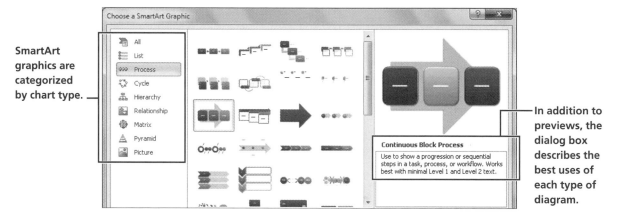

SmartArt graphics are categorized by chart type.

In addition to previews, the dialog box describes the best uses of each type of diagram.

QUICK REFERENCE	USING SMARTART GRAPHIC CHART TYPES
Graphic Category	**Usage**
List	Show nonsequential or grouped blocks of information
Process	Show a progression or sequential flow of data
Cycle	Show a continuing sequence of stages
Hierarchy	Show hierarchal relationships

Graphic Category	Usage
Relationship	Show ideas, show interlocking or overlapping information, or show relationships to a central idea
Matrix	Show the relationships of components to a whole
Pyramid	Show proportional, interconnected, hierarchical, or containment relationships
Picture	Show a variety of information using a central picture or several accent pictures

Example

As you create your presentation, you need to include an organization chart that features the key players in your project or the leadership team of your organization. You give the command to insert a SmartArt Graphic, browse through the Hierarchy list, and then choose an organization chart. You type the various organizational units in the SmartArt's text box. Three minutes later, you're done!

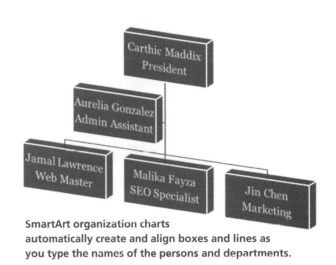

SmartArt organization charts automatically create and align boxes and lines as you type the names of the persons and departments.

QUICK REFERENCE	INSERTING SMARTART
Task	**Procedure**
Insert a new SmartArt graphic	▪ Click the Insert SmartArt Graphic [icon] icon in the center of a slide, or choose Insert→Illustrations→SmartArt from the Ribbon.
	▪ In the Choose a SmartArt Graphic dialog box, select a category of graphics to view the thumbnails and samples.
	▪ Select a thumbnail and click OK.
Edit and format SmartArt	▪ Select the SmartArt graphic (or any shape that is part of the graphic).
	▪ Drag the handles on the shape's border to resize the shape just as you would with clip art.
	▪ Make changes to the color, effects, or layout of the graphic by choosing the various commands on either the SmartArt Tools→Design or SmartArt Tools→Format contextual tabs.
	▪ Reset a SmartArt graphic to its default settings by choosing SmartArt Tools→Design→Reset→Reset Graphic from the Ribbon.
Add a new element to a SmartArt graphic	▪ Select one of the shapes in the SmartArt graphic.
	▪ Choose SmartArt Tools→Design→Create Graphic→Add Shape ▼ menu from the Ribbon and select where you want the new shape to appear relative to the selected shape.

Set Up an Organization Chart

In this exercise, you will create an organization chart in PowerPoint, adding text to the various levels of the chart.

Before You Begin: The iJams presentation should be open.

Insert the Organization Chart

1. Select the **Financial Projections** slide and choose **Home→Slides→New Slide** to insert a new slide.

2. Choose **Home→Slides→** Layout ▾ **→Title and Content** to change the slide's layout.

3. Type **Our Management Team** in the Title placeholder.

4. Click the **Insert SmartArt Graphic** icon in the middle of the slide.
   The Choose a SmartArt Graphic dialog box appears.

5. Follow these steps to insert an organization chart:

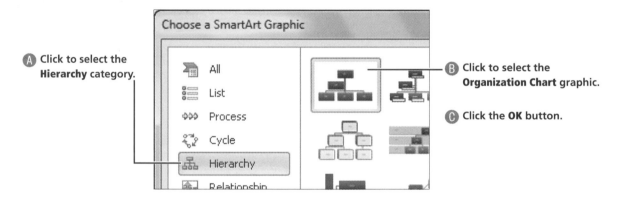

A sample organization chart is inserted. The contextual SmartArt Tools tabs appear on the right side of the Ribbon, including Design and Format.

Add Text

6. Follow these steps to add text to the organization chart:

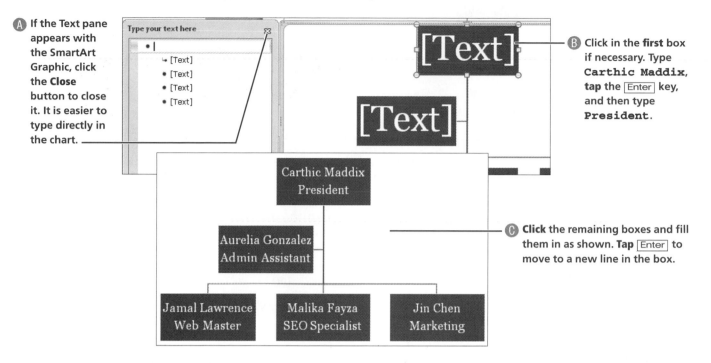

Ⓐ If the Text pane appears with the SmartArt Graphic, click the **Close** button to close it. It is easier to type directly in the chart.

Ⓑ Click in the **first** box if necessary. Type **Carthic Maddix**, tap the [Enter] key, and then type **President**.

Ⓒ **Click** the remaining boxes and fill them in as shown. **Tap** [Enter] to move to a new line in the box.

7. **Save** your presentation and continue with the next topic.

Formatting SmartArt

Video Lesson   labyrinthelab.com/videos

After a SmartArt graphic has been added to a slide, you can format its colors and other effects. For example, you can customize the text formatting, color scheme, and other features of the graphic. Many SmartArt graphics have 3-D schemes and other cool effects you can experiment with to add visual impact to a slide.

Adding Elements to SmartArt

You can also add elements to an original SmartArt graphic. For example, an organization chart might need a new branch for adding a department or lateral relationship. You may insert additional shapes above, below, or next to an existing shape. The SmartArt graphic will automatically resize itself and scale its text to accommodate the extra shapes.

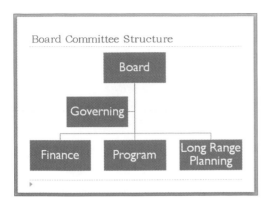
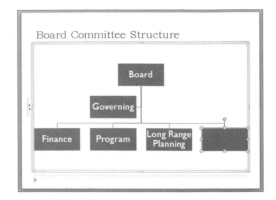

When a shape was inserted below the Board SmartArt, PowerPoint automatically resized the shapes below to make room for the new blank shape.

Add Shapes and Format SmartArt

In this exercise, you will add a new position in the organization chart and enhance its appearance with a different formatting effect.

Add a Coworker Box

1. Click in the **Malika Fayza** box in the organization chart.
   This selects the appropriate box so you can add another shape beside it.

2. Choose **SmartArt Tools→Design→Create Graphic→Add Shape** 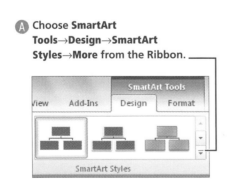 **menu ▼→Add Shape After**.
   A new box is added to the right of the Malika Fayza box and is ready to accept text.

3. Type the name **Brett Schneider** in the new box. Then **tap** Enter to move to a second line in the box and type **Fulfillment**.

Format the Chart

4. Follow these steps to format the chart:

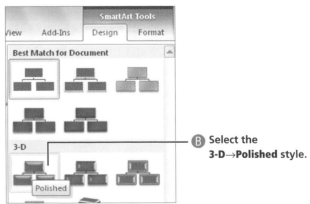

A Choose **SmartArt Tools→Design→SmartArt Styles→More** from the Ribbon.

B Select the **3-D→Polished** style.

The Polished style is applied to every box in the chart. Now the organization chart should resemble the following illustration.

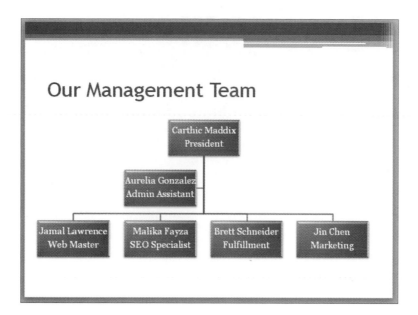

5. **Save** your presentation and **exit** PowerPoint.

4.4 Concepts Review

Concepts Review   labyrinthelab.com/pp10

To check your knowledge of the key concepts introduced in this lesson, complete the Concepts Review quiz by going to the URL listed above. If your classroom is using Labyrinth eLab, you may complete the Concepts Review quiz from within your eLab course.

Reinforce Your Skills

Add a Chart and Change the Chart Type

In this exercise, you will create a new presentation for Tropical Getaways and add a chart slide to the presentation. You will change the chart type to a pie chart.

Begin a New Presentation

1. **Start** PowerPoint. If necessary, choose **File→New** and **double-click** the Blank Presentation icon to create a new blank presentation.

2. Choose **Design→Themes** and select the **Oriel** theme.
   Remember, the themes are listed in alphabetical order. Point to a theme thumbnail and pause for a moment to view the theme name in a pop-up ToolTip.

3. In the **Title** box, type **Tropical Getaways**.

4. Click in the **Subtitle** box and type **Financial Overview**.

Add a Chart Slide and Enter Chart Data

5. Choose **Home→Slides→New Slide** 📋 from the Ribbon and type **2010 Revenue Breakdown** in the title box.

6. Click the **Insert Chart** 📊 icon in the content placeholder box.

7. Choose the **Clustered Column** chart type from the Insert Chart dialog box and click **OK**.

8. Follow these steps to enter data in the chart worksheet:

Ⓐ Change the text in **column A** to **Adventure, Leisure, Family**, and **Singles**.

Ⓑ Change the values in column B to **$800,000, $500,000, $360,000**, and **$620,000**.

◢	A	B	C	D
1		Series 1	Series 2	Series 3
2	Adventure	$800,000	2.4	2
3	Leisure	$500,000	4.4	2
4	Family	$360,000	1.8	3
5	Singles	$620,000	2.8	5

Ⓒ Click in **cell C1**, press and hold ⎇Shift, click in **cell D5**, and release ⎇Shift to select the cells in columns C and D.

Ⓓ Tap ⎀Delete to delete the selected data. The data in columns C and D will be deleted, and the column headers will be renamed to Column1 and Column2. Although the columns still display headers, they will not appear in your graph.

Ⓔ Choose **File→Exit** in the Excel window to exit Excel.

9. Click **once** on the legend to the right of the chart and then **tap** ⎀Delete.

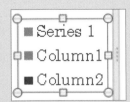

Convert the Chart to a Pie Chart

The data will be easier for attendees to understand if it is graphically represented in a pie chart.

10. With the chart selected, choose **Chart Tools→Design→Type→Change Chart Type** from the Ribbon.

11. If necessary, scroll **down** in the Change Chart Type dialog box to the Pie category and select the **Exploded Pie in 3-D** chart type.

12. Click **OK**, and the graph will now display the data in a pie chart.
The chart displays as a 3-D pie graph, but there are no data labels. You will add data labels in the next activity.

13. **Save** your presentation to your Lesson 04 folder as **Tropical Getaways Overview**.

REINFORCE YOUR SKILLS 4.2

Format a Chart

In this exercise, you will add data labels to a chart. You will also edit the data labels to improve readability.

Before You Begin: The Tropical Getaways Overview presentation you created in the previous exercise should be open.

Format the Pie Chart

In the next few steps, you will remove the chart legend, display data labels, and remove the chart border.

1. If necessary, select the **second slide**, 2010 Revenue Breakdown.

2. **Right-click** any pie piece within the graph and select **Add Data Labels** from the pop-up menu.
The money values are displayed on the pie slices. Next, we will add a text description for each slice.

3. **Right-click** any pie slice in the graph again and choose **Format Data Labels** (not Format Data Series) from the pop-up menu.

4. Follow these steps to format the data labels:

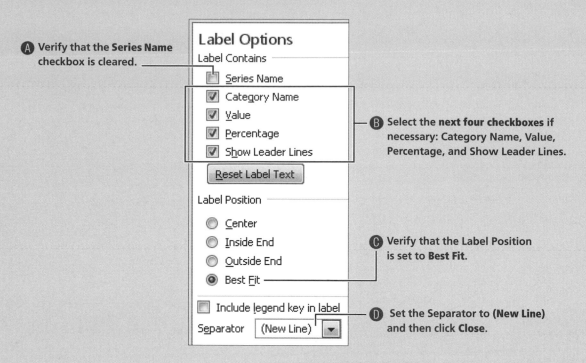

Ⓐ Verify that the **Series Name** checkbox is cleared.

Ⓑ Select the **next four checkboxes** if necessary: Category Name, Value, Percentage, and Show Leader Lines.

Ⓒ Verify that the Label Position is set to **Best Fit**.

Ⓓ Set the Separator to **(New Line)** and then click **Close**.

5. Click **once** on the text *Series 1* above the graph and **tap** [Delete] to remove the chart title.

6. Drag the chart to the lower-left corner of the slide.

7. Drag the **top-right corner** of the chart's border up and to the right until the chart is as large as can be, yet still fits on the slide without obscuring the slide title or document theme graphics.

8. If necessary, choose a different font size from the **Home→Font→ Font Size ▾ menu** on the Ribbon. Your data labels should display on three lines.

9. Save your presentation.

Insert a Chart from a Linked Document

In this exercise, you will link to data in an external document.

Before You Begin: The Tropical Getaways Overview presentation from the previous exercise should be open.

Add a Chart Linked to External Data

1. If necessary, select the **second slide**, 2010 Revenue Breakdown.

2. Choose **Home→Slides→New Slide** from the Ribbon.

3. Choose **Home→Slides→** Layout ▾ **→Title Only** from the Ribbon and type **Revenue Projections** in the title box.
Because we will paste the linked chart, we don't need the placeholder box below the title.

4. Choose **Start→All Programs→Microsoft Office→Microsoft Office Excel 2010** to launch Excel.

5. Choose **File→Open**, navigate to your Lesson 04 folder, and **open** the sb-Tropical Projections spreadsheet.

6. If necessary, **maximize** the Excel window.

7. **Select** the chart and choose **Home→Clipboard→Copy** 📋 from the Ribbon.
   The Excel chart is copied to the computer's Clipboard.

8. **Minimize** Excel.
   Excel minimizes to the taskbar, and the PowerPoint window is visible.

9. Click anywhere **below** the slide title Revenue Projections, and then choose **Home→Clipboard→Paste** from the Ribbon to paste the linked chart.
   The chart is pasted onto the slide. The colors used in the chart may change to match those of your PowerPoint document theme.

10. **Drag** the chart to the lower-left corner of the slide, and then **drag** the chart's top-right border to enlarge the chart as you see fit.

11. Choose **Chart Tools→Design→Type→Change Chart Type** 📊 from the Ribbon, and then select the **Clustered Cylinder** type and click **OK**.

12. Choose **Home→Font→Font Size ▾ menu→18**.

13. **Save** your presentation and choose **File→Exit**.

Edit the Data

In the next few steps, you will edit the data in the linked document and refresh the chart data.

14. **Restore** Excel from the taskbar and **maximize** the window if necessary.

15. Change the value of **cell E4** (the Family in 2013 cell) to **3.6**.

16. Choose **File→Save** to save changes to the worksheet.

17. Choose **File→Exit** to close Excel.

18. Choose **Start→All Programs→Microsoft Office→Microsoft Office PowerPoint 2010**.

19. Choose **File→Recent→Tropical Getaways Overview** from the top of the Recent Documents pane.

20. Select the **third slide**, Revenue Projections, and select the chart.
    Notice the old value for Family in 2013 is still displayed.

21. Choose **Chart Tools→Design→Data→Refresh Data** 🔄 from the Ribbon.
    The value for Family in 2013 now displays the updated value.

22. **Save** your presentation.

Add an Organization Chart and Closing Slide

In this exercise, you will add an organization chart to the Tropical Getaways Overview presentation.

Before You Begin: The Tropical Getaways Overview presentation from the previous exercise folder should be open.

1. If necessary, select the **last slide** in the presentation, Revenue Projections.
2. Choose **Home→Slides→New Slide** 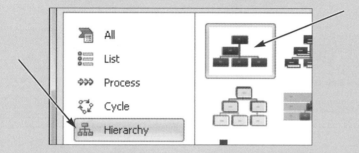 to insert a new slide.
3. Choose **Home→Slides→** Layout ▾ **→Title and Content** to change the slide layout.
4. **Type** the title **Our Team**.
5. Click the **Insert SmartArt Graphic** icon in the middle of the slide.
6. Choose the **Hierarchy** category on the left side of the Choose a SmartArt Graphic dialog box. Then choose the **Organization Chart** thumbnail and click **OK**.

7. **Enter** the following text into the organization chart:

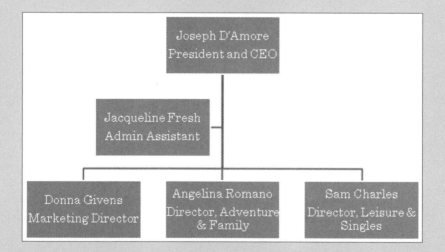

8. Select the **Sam Charles** box and choose **SmartArt Tools→Design→Create Graphic→Add Shape ▾→Add Shape After** from the Ribbon.
   A new shape is added, and the SmartArt Graphic resizes itself to accommodate the additional box.

9. In the new box, type **Jerome Sakai** Enter **Customer Service**.
10. Choose **Home→Slides→New Slide** from the Ribbon.

11. Choose **Home**→**Slides**→ ▦ Layout ▾ →**Section Header** from the Ribbon.

12. Give the slide a title of **Tropical Getaways** and a subtitle of **Our Destination Is Success**.

13. Choose **Slide Show**→**Start Slide Show**→**From Beginning** 🖳 from the Ribbon and navigate through the presentation until you return to Normal view.

14. **Save** your changes and **close** the presentation.

Apply Your Skills

Insert and Format an Embedded Chart

In this exercise, you will add and format a chart in the Classic Cars BoD presentation.

1. **Open** the as-Classic Cars BoD presentation from your Lesson 04 folder

2. Select the **second slide**, Top Income Sources of 2010.

Add a Chart

3. Click the **Insert Chart** icon in the placeholder, select the **Clustered Cone** chart type, and create a datasheet with the entries shown.

	A	B	C	D
1		Trade Shows	Internet Sales	Infomercials
2	Q1	1.4	0.5	0.9
3	Q2	1.5	0.7	0.8
4	Q3	2.5	0.9	1.2
5	Q4	2	1	1

4. After entering data, **close** the datasheet to return to the PowerPoint slide.

5. Choose **Chart Tools→Design→Chart Layouts→Layout 2** and change the chart's default title, *Chart Title*, to **Millions of Dollars per Quarter**.

6. Click the chart's **border** to select the entire chart, and then choose **Home→Font→Bold** to make all the chart text bold and easier to see from a distance.

7. Click anywhere **outside** of the chart and take a moment to examine the chart options you just set.

8. **Save** your presentation and continue with the next exercise.

Insert and Format a Linked Chart

In this exercise, you will add and format a chart in the Classic Cars BoD presentation.

Before You Begin: The Classic Cars BoD presentation from the previous exercise should be open.

1. **Start** Excel and **open** the as-Classic Cars Projections spreadsheet from your Lesson 04 folder.

2. **Copy** the chart to the Clipboard and **exit** Excel.

3. Insert a **new slide** at the end of the presentation and change the slide layout to **Title Only**.

4. Type **2011 Financial Projections** for the slide title.

5. **Paste** the chart on the slide.

6. Change the chart type to a **Clustered Pyramid** and change its layout to **Layout 2**.

7. **Resize** the chart so it is as large as can be without obscuring the slide title.

8. Change the chart's title to read **Projected Earnings in Millions** and set the font size for all chart text to size **18**.

9. **Save** your presentation and continue with the next exercise.

Insert an Organization Chart

In this exercise, you will add and format a chart in the Classic Cars BoD presentation.

Before You Begin: The Classic Cars BoD presentation from the previous exercise should be open.

1. Insert a **new slide** at the end and change its layout to **Title and Content**.

2. Add the title **Who Will Get Us There?**

3. Develop the **organization chart** by adding the boxes and text shown in the following illustration. Start with the default **Hierarchy List** SmartArt graphic and add shapes as needed.

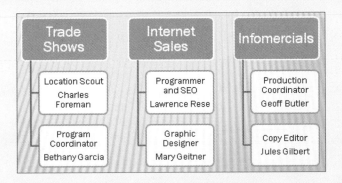

4. **Save** the changes to your presentation and **exit** PowerPoint.

Critical Thinking & Work-Readiness Skills

In the course of working through the following Microsoft Office-based Critical Thinking exercises, you will also be utilizing various work-readiness skills, some of which are listed next to each exercise. Go to labyrinthelab.com/ workreadiness to learn more about the work-readiness skills.

4.1 Link and Format an Excel Chart

In preparation for a loan application, Carthic and Aurelia brainstorm questions bankers might ask. One likely question is, who is your competition? Jin, iJams' marketing analyst, has created an Excel spreadsheet indicating the market saturation of your competitors. Open the presentation ct-iJams Is Growing and the Excel spreadsheet ct-Competition (Lesson 04 folder). Copy and paste the Excel chart to the appropriate PowerPoint slide. Save the presentation as **ct-iJams Loan**. Close the Excel spreadsheet. Change the chart type to one of the pie charts and apply a chart style to add punch. Save your changes. If working in a group, discuss your choice of key points and format. If working alone, type your answer in a Word document named **ct-Questions** saved to your Lesson 04 folder.

4.2 Add an Organizational Chart

Another question Carthic and Aurelia think they might be asked is, what makes you successful? Start with the ct-iJams Loan presentation you created in the previous exercise and save it to your Lesson 04 folder with the new name **ct-iJams Success**. Insert a SmartArt graphic on the final slide that illustrates a progression of steps or ideas, such as one from the Process category. Fill in the chart with phrases of best business practices, such as "world class customer service" or "quality products." Experiment with changing the SmartArt graphic to different types until you find one that fits the slide theme and phrases. Apply a style of your choice to add visual interest to the graphic. Save your changes.

4.3 Edit External Data

Aurelia asks Carthic, "What if our competition changes?" Save the ct-iJams Success presentation you created in the previous lesson to your Lesson 04 folder as **ct-iJams Updated Competition**. Edit the linked chart data to show Joe Diamond Recording has decreased to 30 percent and a brand new competitor, Silverlake Studios, has acquired 15 percent of the market saturation. Verify the new data is displayed on the PowerPoint chart. Save your changes. Open the ct-iJams Loan presentation you created in the first exercise and display the linked Excel chart. Does the chart on this older presentation display the new Excel data? Why or why not? Type your answers in a Word document named **ct-Questions2** saved to your Lesson 04 folder.

Index

Notes

Notes

Notes

Notes

Notes